THE

SUBVERSIVE

COPY EDITOR

Chicago Guides
to *Writing*, Editing,
and Publishing

THE
SUBVERSIVE
COPY EDITOR

ADVICE FROM CHICAGO

(OR, HOW TO NEGOTIATE GOOD
RELATIONSHIPS WITH YOUR WRITERS,
YOUR COLLEAGUES, AND YOURSELF)

Carol Fisher Saller

THE UNIVERSITY OF CHICAGO PRESS

Chicago and London

Carol Fisher Saller is a senior manuscript editor at the University of Chicago Press and editor of the *Chicago Manual of Style Online*'s Q&A.

The University of Chicago Press, Chicago 60637
The University of Chicago Press, Ltd., London
© 2009 by Carol Fisher Saller
All rights reserved. Published 2009
Printed in the United States of America

18 17 16 15 14 13 12 11 10 09   2 3 4 5

ISBN-13: 978-0-226-73424-8 (cloth)
ISBN-10: 0-226-73424-2 (cloth)
ISBN-13: 978-0-226-73425-5 (paper)
ISBN-10: 0-226-73425-0 (paper)

Library of Congress Cataloging-in-Publication Data

Saller, Carol.
    The subversive copy editor : advice from Chicago (or, how to negotiate good relationships with your writers, your colleagues, and yourself) / Carol Fisher Saller.
        p.   cm.—(Chicago guides to writing, editing, and publishing)
    Includes bibliographical references and index.
    ISBN-13: 978-0-226-73424-8 (cloth : alk. paper)
    ISBN-10: 0-226-73424-2 (cloth : alk. paper)
    ISBN-13: 978-0-226-73425-5 (pbk. : alk. paper)
    ISBN-10: 0-226-73425-0 (pbk. : alk. paper) 1. Copy editing. I. Title.
    PN4784.C75S25   2009
    808'.06607—dc22

                                                                    2008031055

No passion in the world is equal to

the passion to alter someone else's draft.

H. G. WELLS

Contents

Introduction

I hear you.

As the editor of the *Chicago Manual of Style*'s monthly Q&A, I've been reading your questions about writing style since the University of Chicago Press launched the Q&A in 1997. That amounts to tens of thousands of queries from students, professors, copy editors, businesspeople, and writers who struggle as they write and edit. As of this writing, the *Chicago Manual of Style Online* website receives about two million visitors per month, and the Q&A is the most frequently visited page. Fortunately for us, most of those visitors do not submit questions.

The Chicago Manual of Style, for the uninitiated, is one of the English-speaking world's most revered style manuals. Although Chicago style may not have the most users, it surely has the most devoted. From its beginnings in the 1890s as a simple in-house sheet of proofreading tips for manuscript editors at the University of Chicago Press to its current CD-ROM, online, and print editions, it has grown into a bible for writers and editors in almost every kind of writing outside journalism (where Associated Press style and *New York Times* style dominate).

Written by the Manuscript Editing Department at the University of Chicago Press (where I work), the *Manual of Style* has chapters on everything from punctuation and capitalization to mathematics and foreign languages. Its chapters on documentation (the styling of notes and bibliographies) have been adopted by universities around the world. Users of *CMOS* include the most impossibly learned writers and editors as well as the most clueless, and for more than a decade the monthly Q&A has played host to them all.

Reading the questions that come through the site is a daily adventure away from editing tasks. We answer as many as we can, and I choose the best ones for the monthly posting. The range of topics can be startling. Here's a note we received from the Jet Propulsion Laboratory at NASA:

· Dear *Chicago Manual of Style* Q&A Person: What is the rule for sequencing adjectives in a series? For example, we know that numbers come before size indicators (e.g., six small apples). We also know that colors come after size indicators (e.g., six small yellow apples). The specific problem is whether to say "narrow anticyclonically dominated northwestern coast" or "anticyclonically dominated narrow northwestern coast." (Please don't say the correct answer is "anticyclonically dominated northwestern narrow coast"!)

And their kicker ending: "What is the rule that supports your answer?"[1]

In contrast, another rather dreamy-sounding note read simply, "Dear *CMOS*, What is Chicago style? Could you give an example?" And one of my favorites: "Dear Chicago, Hello—my question is how can I find student apartments for the area of Northeastern Illinois University? I have checked, but I can't seem to find apartments a full-time student could afford. Thanks so much."

---

1. Our reply, after consultation with a linguist: "Our consultant was somewhat hesitant to comment without a fuller context to work with, suspecting that this may be a 'sentence-level issue and not an adjective-phrase-level issue.' He pointed out that sequencing can vary for reasons of emphasis and that without having the context, he couldn't discern the intended emphasis. If 'narrow' is the emphasis, then it should come first (followed by a comma). If 'anticyclonically dominated' is the emphasis, then it should come first (followed by a comma)."

Questions come from all over the world, some from readers who struggle with English. Their grammar questions go deep and are beyond our ability to respond. ("Please tell differences of *at* and *to*.") A professor wrote from Beijing to say that he was translating the *Manual* into Chinese because he perceived a need for it there. (I can hardly wait to see what kinds of questions we receive once *CMOS* is available in Chinese.)

Most of the messages I read, however, are basic questions about style. Often I know the answer, but sometimes I have to look it up—or I e-mail my fellow manuscript editors in the department for a quick consensus, or I run around and ask the first two or three colleagues I can find. Although people outside the Press address us "Dear style goddesses" and assume we are experts on everything in the *Manual*, most of the time I feel more like the pathetic little person behind the curtain in *The Wizard of Oz*. It's only because I'm surrounded and protected by knowledgeable and generous coworkers that I can assemble the authoritative front that appears in the Q&A. When I get an esoteric question involving technical writing or linguistics, I phone or e-mail one of the professors on campus for help. If a question is clearly outside the purview of the *CMOS* help site, I sometimes do an Internet search and point the reader to a more relevant site.

For the most frequently asked questions, I keep template replies that I can personalize. I can't count the number of times we've been asked whether to type one space or two at the end of a sentence (it's one) or how to cite a TV commercial (this always worries me a little). And I keep the links to Etiquette Hell and Grammar Girl handy.[2] The monthly Q&A that I cull from all these exchanges is always read by my managing editor and at least two other colleagues, who correct my grammar and punctuation and tactfully set me straight when something is wrong.

Some people write back to thank us, which can be more or less gratifying. ("I'm thrilled to receive wisdom from the horse's mouth"; or "Thanks so much for the swift reply. I was a little disappointed at

2. http://etiquettehell.com; http://grammar.qdnow.com/.

the lack of humor, though.") I'm always tempted to respond briefly to these ("No problem—yours, Trigger"; or "Sorry—I couldn't decide whether to laugh or cry"), but I rarely do, for fear of acquiring a few too many new best friends.

Two categories of questions seem to make up the bulk of the mail, and they're the ones that inspired me to write this book. The first type comes from readers who want us to settle an argument. From these questions I hear a persistent cry of frustration:

- I know I'm right about something. Could *CMOS* please confirm it?
- I know I'm right about something. Could you please set my teacher/ student/author/colleague/boss/editor straight?
- I know I'm right about something. Could you please save the English-speaking world from its slide into illiteracy?

The second main category of questions comes from writers or editors who are struggling to finish a project and have hit a wall:

- My deadline was yesterday, so please hurry with your reply.
- I've finished the editing, and here is a list of all the things I haven't figured out yet. Could you help?
- How would you edit this bibliography? (Just do the first ten—I can take it from there.)

This book is for all of you: those students, professors, copy editors, businesspeople, and writers who are sometimes dogged by indecision or confusion over rules of style and grammar; for those of you who know the rules but agonize over when or whether to apply them; for those who copyedit for a living and those who don't and those who would like to. In the following pages, I hope to soothe and encourage and lend power. I am not going to do this, however, by setting your teacher/student/author/colleague/boss/editor straight. And I'm not going to help with your homework. You won't learn the fundamentals of copyediting from me. Rather, consider this a "relationship" book, because I'm going to talk about the main relationships in your work life—with the writer, with your colleagues, and with yourself—in ways that you might not have considered before. Ways that might be called subversive.

Right away I should explain what I do *not* mean by a "subversive copy editor," in case anyone has in mind a character like the one my colleague Joe Weintraub once described in a prize-winning short story. In the story, a snooty language expert named Ezra Peckinpah has been tormented for months by a copy editor who purposely inserts errors into his column at the final stage before printing. In this scene, Ezra has just received the latest issue:

> He held the issue up to the light as if he were inspecting the texture of the paper itself for flaws, and when he found himself beginning the final paragraph with the ungrammatical apostrophe "Just between you, dear reader, and I . . ." his arms twitched outward, his elbow striking his reading lamp so that it tottered on its base and almost toppled to the floor.
>
> "Galleys!" he screamed into the telephone. "I demand to see galleys!"[3]

No—at the risk of disappointing my more twisted readers, let me clarify up front that my subversive copy editor is an entirely different creature.

Subversive, first, because this editor overthrows the popular view that the writer is a natural adversary, competing for power over the prose. In part 1 of this book, I will lay out an alternate view and suggest what I believe to be the most productive order of an editor's loyalties, an order that puts the writer closer to the top of the list and (don't tell my boss) the publishing house closer to the bottom, as they work together in the service of the reader.

Subversive, second, because to live a good life as a copy editor, this editor must occasionally think outside the rules. To copyedit is to confront and solve an endless series of problems, great and small. In part

3. Joe Weintraub, "The Well of English, Defiled," *Ascent* 10, no. 1 (Fall 1984): 43–57.

2 of the book, in examining the copy editor's life of conflict, I will zero in on some of the ways we create problems for ourselves even when our writers are expert, thorough, and compliant. You will see how a need to always cleave to the rules can be counterproductive. I will seek to banish the pet compulsions, inflexibilities, and superstitions that get in our way. More than once in these pages, you will read the heretical idea "It's not a matter of being correct or incorrect. It's only a style."

In explaining this theme to my son John, I said I wanted to find ways for all parties to get what they want, sometimes by breaking the rules, and John asked, "Oh—like shoplifting?" Well, no. The idea isn't to allow bad grammar and sloppy attribution of sources. The idea of a good author-editor relationship involves working with the writer in ways that will tell you what he really wants so you can help him achieve it. A great deal of the time, you'll find that what the writer wants, you want, too. And if you're skilled, the writer will discover that he wants most of the same things you do. The second idea, of having a good relationship with our colleagues and ourselves as copy editors, involves forming work habits and attitudes that allow us to complete our tasks having done the best we can do with the material we were given, without sacrificing more than a little bit of our standards, our sanity, or our sleep.

And who knows? If we're lucky, in the course of figuring out some strategies for getting along with our authors, our bosses, our colleagues, and ourselves, we might also happen to learn something more about getting along in life.

· · ·

I am a working manuscript editor at the University of Chicago Press,[4] which publishes scholarly books in a wide variety of disciplines. My

4. At the risk of enraging some readers, I will use the terms "copy editor" and "manuscript editor" interchangeably. Although their definitions vary, in my mind they are overlapping terms. "Copyediting" is done by many workers who are not primarily editors—it involves the more or less mechanical reading of copy for spelling, grammar, logic, style, consistency, and appropriate expression. Depending on the worker's level of responsibility, it can be restricted to those functions or allow for greater engagement with the work. "Manuscript editing" is the work of professional editors. It includes copyediting but also

work keeps me in daily contact with people in acquisitions, design, production, and marketing as we go through the mechanics of making books. Although there are fourteen full-time manuscript editors on staff, we aren't enough to handle all the books, so we use freelance copy editors as well. Almost all of the editing is done electronically, and although my colleagues and I share tips and tricks, at Chicago there's no rigid standard operating procedure for the preparation of disks or for the copyediting of books. This gives us an autonomy that we all prize; in this book I will try to keep in mind that not all copy editors are working on books; you aren't all working in-house; you don't all have the same flexibility to balk at rules. I devote one chapter to the special concerns of freelancers.

In the Manuscript Editing Department at Chicago, although most of us have higher degrees, we don't tend to specialize in particular subjects. Manuscripts are usually assigned on the basis of schedule and availability. Over the years, I've landed a three-volume work on the vertebrate skull, a book of Jewish jokes, and a seven-hundred-page bibliography of historical geography. Literary criticism, art history, ethnomusicology, gay and lesbian studies—we edit everything except math and the physical sciences, which we send to specialist freelancers. (I once supervised a freelancer who read *Quantum Field Theory in Curved Spacetime and Black Hole Thermodynamics*, a book I kept on my shelf for years to impress visitors.)

Although the bulk of my experience has been in the editing of scholarly book manuscripts, I have also worked in trade publishing and journalism, and indeed long ago as a secretary, a clerk/typist, in data entry, and (just for the record) as a letter carrier. In all of those jobs, I was responsible for writing or editing—or carrying—copy. All this is only to say that I've edited a lot of words and learned a few things along the way that I'd like to share, because you are asking.

---

encompasses larger responsibilities of handling copy through several stages of production; it may also entail deeper engagement with the content: rethinking, rewriting. In the rare case of one of my projects, my queries about documentation led to abandonment of the project altogether.

In our mail, we tend to hear from the frustrated, the panicked, the disaffected. But I like to believe that when we're *not* hearing from you, it's because you're doing just fine, enjoying the pleasures of working at your craft. Knowing how to tinker with a broken piece of prose until it hums is a source of contentment known by all who have mastered a worthy craft. The midwife works with a laboring woman to produce a healthy child. A seamstress or tailor finishes the couturier's garment until it's a perfect, flattering fit. Carpenters and masons execute an architect's vision and take pride in a safe and well-functioning building. What we all have in common is our wish to cooperate—not compete—with the originators of our material, and we share a satisfaction and sense of accomplishment when everything is going well.

Ultimately, I'm hopeful that a reexamination of your role as copy editor can benefit all parties while liberating you from the oppression of unhelpful habits and attitudes. My point is not how to copyedit, but how to survive while doing it. My hope is to give you some self-assurance and a measure of grace as you go about negotiating one word at a time with the writers you are charged with saving from themselves.

PART ONE

WORKING WITH THE WRITER, FOR THE READER

CHAPTER ONE

The Subversive Copy Editor

Q / My author wants his preface to come at the end of the book. This just seems ridiculous to me. I mean, it's not a *post*-face.

WHO ARE YOU?

From reading the letters to the Q&A, I'm guessing that many readers of this book are not professional copy editors. But that doesn't mean you don't copyedit. In the routines of almost any office job, a worker is likely to be responsible for a chunk of writing, and in any chunk of writing there is likely to be a problem. Solving problems with writing is what copyediting is. The periodical called *Copy Editor* recently changed its name to *Copyediting*, reasoning that "the number of those who bear the title 'copy editor' decreases year on year." Editor Wendalyn Nichols explains that "more corporations are developing custom publications, and editorial freelancers are branching out beyond the niches they could once remain in quite comfortably. Increasingly, people who edit copy must wear more than one hat."[1] Perhaps as a result, much of the Q&A mail is from workers who aren't trained to copyedit and are looking for guidance.

Anyone who works with the words of others can benefit from

1. Wendalyn Nichols, "Ask *Copy Editor*," in *Copy Editor*, August–September 2007, 4.

advice to professional copy editors. Although I will tend to use the vocabulary I know best, that of a copy editor of book manuscripts, the same tenets can apply in the multitude of contexts where you handle copy written by others, whether for publication or not: newspapers and magazines, corporate and nonprofit materials, online content, newsletters, advertisements, comic books, love letters . . . well, maybe not love letters. Regardless of your title, I invite you to read on.

WHO'S THE BOSS?

When you're faced with a chunk of writing to tame, you sit with your favorite dictionary, *Words into Type*, *The Chicago Manual of Style* or another style guide, and any other references you use to guide your editing. You might sit in an office with six sharpened pencils on your desk. Or in a basement room, with pizza oozing grease onto the hard copy. You're armed with your own training and inclinations. Maybe your delete-key finger is itching to stab at extra *thats*; maybe you laser in on punctuation. Or maybe you're the big-picture type, ready to put paragraph 1 at the end and write the opener from scratch.

Regardless of your modus operandi, when you start in on the process of reading the words and making editorial decisions, you have in mind at least vaguely and sometimes quite clearly an end product that will take a certain form and meet a certain standard. Not necessarily your own, alas. Rather, you are bound to adhere to the standard set by the person or institution that is producing the work and—need I say—paying you for your time.

And that is simply wrong.

Don't be alarmed: I'm not going to suggest that you toss out your stylebook and forget what you know about semicolons and dangling modifiers. On the contrary, I'm going to insist that you know these things inside and out. And no, I don't mean that the person you're ultimately aiming to satisfy is the writer. Who's left—yourself? Of course not. What I am suggesting is that your first loyalty be to the audience of the work you're editing: that is, the reader.

I know you saw that coming. Common sense tells us that working on behalf of the reader is not really such a terribly subversive move. After all, that is the mission of the publisher in the first place, even if only for the obvious reason that pleasing readers sells the book, the magazine, the newspaper. Persuading readers creates business. Reassuring and impressing readers keeps them coming back. Since most publishers court some variety in their readers, and most institutions create documents for various purposes, it makes sense that editors will have to tailor their efforts accordingly. And when you do that, it's likely that at some point you're going to have to butt heads with the writer.

Indeed, editing for the reader routinely involves questioning established rules of style. How could it not? The style of an article written about the naked mole rat will not be appropriate for one written about, well, copy editors. Although the fundamental elements of well-crafted prose are basically the same for all writing, the details are not. A word like "pre-dewatering" can be workaday jargon in a memo about waste treatment, or a witticism in a poem for the *New Yorker*. Numbers like seven thousand three hundred and sixty-two may look fine in a novel but would get out of hand in a math book. Humor doesn't always fit. Repetition can be necessary for emphasis or organization, or it can just be annoying.

But jettisoning a style rule or tenet of good writing doesn't have to mean sacrificing excellence. Rather, it can ensure it. Examples are legion. Here's one: some style guides dictate that upon first mention, a person be identified by a full name. In news articles, trade books, or school texts destined for readers of mixed abilities and attention spans, the goal is to include the uninitiated and educate them. Adding William to Shakespeare or Margaret to Thatcher isn't likely to insult anyone and will allow a broader base of readers to follow the text without confusion. In specialized or technical documents, however, directed to a narrow group of experts, a writer might prefer the shorthand of the familiar name alone. In an offhand reference to Dante, she doesn't want to add the gratuitous Alighieri; a good writer knows she would only patronize readers by belaboring the obvious. Dante will do.

Although it's likely that you'll need to tinker with a writer's prose in order to shape it for the intended reader, you shouldn't automatically expect a major overhaul. Although there are always going to be writers who need reminding whom they're writing for, fortunately for you, most writers are likely to be better acquainted than you are with the special readership of their work, and you would do well to think before you mess with their choices.

And that brings us to the next issue.

WHOSE MANUSCRIPT IS IT, ANYWAY?

It's good to assume at the outset that a writer has written with her imagined reader in mind. If your writer is an expert, whatever her specialty—computer technology, poetry, fashion—she'll have been steeping in the jargon of that discipline for a long time, and she's bound to use it, knowing that it's the best way to communicate with readers who speak the same dialect. Even if she's only recently researched the subject for a commissioned piece, she probably knows more than you do about it. In that way, the writer has already put her reader first, and now she can reasonably expect the editing process to push her manuscript a little further in the same direction. In her fantasies, your editing will produce a perfect, fascinating work of art. (In her nightmares, you will reduce her work to rubble, but never mind that.) Considering the responsibility this entails, then, let the writer become your second master.

One of the most counterproductive assumptions for young editors to make is that they are going to be working against the recalcitrance of writers who are ignorant of the rules. Copy editors are often trained in this attitude. They are taught how to say no to authors, employing the vocabulary of rule enforcement—it's unconventional; it's not our style; it's too expensive; it will cause a delay. Sometimes, as a last resort, we do deploy those weapons. But to see the author-editor relationship as inherently adversarial is to doom yourself to a career of angst and stress. The writer's job is far more difficult than the copy editor's; she has to actually write the thing. It is your privilege to polish a manuscript without the tedium and agony of producing it in the first place. Your first goal isn't to slash and burn your way through in an effort to make it conform to a list of style rules. Your first goal is merely to do no harm.

And oh, baby—the ways in which we do harm.

For every writer with a tin ear who is helped by a competent editor, there is surely an inexperienced editor who will take a fresh and well-voiced text and edit the life out of it. He'll delete every comma that isn't justified in his high school grammar, and he'll put them in where the writer is trying to pick up speed. He will create tortuous constructions to avoid a preposition at the end of a sentence, and he would lay down his life to keep an infinitive intact. For such editors, the task of imposing consistency extends beyond the stylings that give a reader ease and confidence in the writer's authority. These types are obsessed with imposing rules—sometimes rules that are closer to superstitions—that serve only to hamstring the writer and impoverish his prose. It's no wonder that they see the writer as a roadblock on the way to the straightened texts they work to achieve.

You might think that the overachieving copy editor suffers from knowing too much, but the opposite is true. Knowing too little, she hangs on white-knuckled to her small bag of tricks, unaware of the many alternatives. So the first step in doing no harm is to expand your bag of tricks. A thorough knowledge of the rules and conventions of prose styling will arm you with confidence in choosing the right ones and rejecting the wrong ones. There's a difference between the considered breaking of a rule and a failure to observe it out of ignorance. In the former case, you will have a reason and a plan; in the latter, you might just have a mess. You could find yourself blanching at a headline like "Press Recalls Typo-Filled Book and Says It Will Reprint."[2]

So if you aren't trained and confident in at least the basics of copyediting, or if you're charged with following a style guide that you

2. *Chronicle of Higher Education News Blog*, article posted May 2, 2008, http://chronicle
.com/news/index.php?id=4427&utm_source=pm&utm_medium=en (accessed May 2,
2008).

haven't mastered, you can't hope to give the readers what they deserve—or gain the respect of your writer.[3] Knowing your stuff, you're ready to serve the reader by working intelligently and sensitively with the writer.

When you receive a work ready for copyediting, you, more than anyone else, are in a position to champion the writer and protect her project. Nobody else cares as much as you do about that particular work at that particular time. It's likely that none of your colleagues will read its final version. The editor who acquired it has been there and done that—he's on to courting the next deal. The manager or assigning editor thumbed through it and signed it off to you. The marketer is thinking about it as part of a greater plan; the print buyer isn't engaged with its content much at all. Who, if not you, will be the writer's advocate? If there's a problem—if the fiscal-year projections can't be revised in time, if a book index is too long—everyone benefits if you are thinking of the project as your own and pushing to get the best of everything for it.

WHY WE MEDDLE

People uninitiated in the publishing process might be surprised to learn that there is even such a thing as the copyediting stage. Don't writers proofread and polish and revise before the text is even submitted in the first place? Don't acquiring editors critique and send manuscripts to outside readers and push the authors to refine and update on the basis of the feedback? Isn't the darned thing practically perfect by then?

---

3. There are many ways to acquire knowledge of copyediting through reading books and articles about it, but experience is, as in most undertakings, the best teacher. If you have yet to find work copyediting, check out some of the books and online resources recommended in the "Further Reading" section and consider taking a course in manuscript editing. Find some pro bono work—edit a friend's dissertation (preferably not your best friend's) and get feedback from the writer. And see the appendix to this book, on how to get your foot in the door to a copyediting career.

Well, no.

In academic publishing, a manuscript probably goes through more versions, more outside review, and more refining than any other kind of copy by the time it gets to the copy editor. But even so, when an author and her peers read a manuscript, they tend to focus on the larger picture, the argument, the logic, the organization, and the clarity or accuracy of expression. They will point out misspellings or grammar goofs or inconsistencies if they spot them, but that isn't their mission. A manuscript editor keeps an eye on all that, but he is also taking careful notes and cross-checking hundreds of details. He is going to notice that footnote 43 cites page 12 of a particular article in the *American Journal of Sociology*, whereas the bibliography entry for that article indicates that the article begins on page 22. He's recording in his style sheet that Edward Mulholland appears on page 51 and is going to be suspicious when *Edwin* Mulholland pops up on page 372. He's the one who will find three different spellings of Tchaikowsky/Tchaikovsky/Tchaikovski and that chapter 3 is titled "The Untruth of the Gaze" in the table of contents but "The Untrue Gaze" at the chapter's opening.[4]

In other kinds of publishing, copy will come to you having undergone much less scrutiny than a book manuscript. A news story may have been madly typed that morning by a stringer on the train into the office. Your boss could hand you a letter to potential donors written with a Sharpie on the wrapper from her lunch burrito. You may have to start with larger tasks of rewriting before moving on to the finer points of spelling, punctuation, and internal consistency.

Now I know there are readers among you—maybe those who are only just beginning to contemplate work as a copy editor—who are wondering, "How much does any of this really matter?"

---

4. Copy editors keep a separate style sheet for every document they edit in order to keep track of decisions that depart from the default style. The classic arrangement is alphabetical (with separate sections for numbers, punctuation, etc.), so we can refer to the sheet and find what we're looking for. If we allow a hyphen in *post-war*, it goes under the letter *p*. Proofreaders must have a copy of the style sheet of whatever they proof. Otherwise they might start undoing the editor's work.

The publishers who hire copy editors obviously believe that it matters a lot. It matters because inaccuracies and inconsistencies undermine a writer's authority, distract and confuse the reader, and reflect poorly on the company. If a page number in the table of contents is wrong, the data in table 4 is just as likely to be wrong. If Goran Visnjic's name is misspelled, who's going to believe he actually gave the interview? Discriminating readers look for reasons to trust a writer and reasons not to. Inelegant expression and carelessness in the details are two reasons not to. The copy editor's job, then, is to ferret out the remaining infelicities in a manuscript. We do this in order to help the writer forge a connection with the reader based on trust—trust that the writer is intelligent and responsible, and that her work is a reliable source. We do it to help craft an article that pleases, a report that allows the reader to coast along through its ideas without slowing for red lights at every corner. And we do it—don't we?—because we derive satisfaction and pride from knowing how.

As you read, you will listen for the writer's voice and become her imagined reader, mentally connecting the style of her prose to the message of her pages. You will learn to want what she wants, and you will edit to keep her from wandering off the path. When you perceive that what she wants in the moment gets in the way of her greater goals, that's when you step in.

I realize that some copy editors are never given an opportunity to communicate with the writers of the materials they edit. Although this arrangement does have its advantages, it obviously prevents you from following some of the advice in the first four chapters of this book. I hope you will find the book—and even those chapters—helpful in any case. You too have a relationship with your writers, and it can be combative or collaborative, as you wish. You too can wish to do no harm; you too can listen for the writer's voice and work to protect and promote it.

With this in mind, let's lay the groundwork for an excellent author-editor relationship.

A / Figure out (perhaps by asking) why the author doesn't want the preface up front. Maybe it gives away a surprising conclusion. Maybe it slows down the reader. Contemplate this. If you can agree that the author is right about the placement, point out that the title "Preface" is inaccurate, and ask whether he wants to call it an epilogue, conclusion, afterword, or something else. In the unlikely event that he insists on calling it a preface, keep pressing. Point out your fear that the misnomer will strike readers as an error of ignorance. Admit that you're afraid they'll see it as an editorial error. Ask him to add a note explaining his whim. Don't give up; in the end, you'll work something out that satisfies you both.

CHAPTER TWO

The Good Launch

Q / The menu in our cafeteria shows that enchiladas are available
"Tues.–Fri." However, when I ordered one on a Wednesday, I was informed
that enchiladas are available on Tuesday *and* Friday, not Tuesday *through*
Friday. When I informed the cafeteria manager that this was incorrect,
she seemed shocked and refused to change the sign. Please help determine
who is correct!

THREE VIRTUES OF THE ENLIGHTENED EDITOR

When you are given a manuscript to edit, that manuscript comes with
a writer attached. Sometimes you're allowed to ignore this fact: the
copy will be published without a byline, the writer has little invested
in the copy, or author-editor contact will be nil. (Think movie listings
in the community newspaper, or next month's lunch menus for the
company bulletin boards.) Sometimes, in contrast, you have edited
the same writer for years, and you have become, for better or for worse,
helpmate, adviser, coconspirator. (Think the CEO whose letters you
type, or the staff writers or columnists for your newspaper or magazine.) If your editor-writer relationships are of these types—dead-end
or committed—you may skip ahead. This chapter is all about when
you are thrown together with a new writer and have to figure out how
to get along.

Now that I think about it, contacting a writer for the first time is much like answering a personals ad, except that you can be honest. Especially in book editing, it's unusual for a manuscript editor to know the writer beforehand, and in many instances, perhaps most, they never meet in person. Why should he trust you with his magnum opus? Right off the bat, you will give him three reasons: (1) because your introductory letter or e-mail or phone call shows that you are careful, (2) because you are going to make the process transparent, and (3) because you show no signs of the editorial inflexibility that terrifies writers. *Carefulness*, *transparency*, and *flexibility*: put these words on your little rubber bracelet. We shall return to them more than once.

Write or e-mail after you've looked over the project but before you start editing. The writer is going to be your best ally as you work, so establish cordial relations. Introduce yourself and explain your role in the publishing process. Show that you've familiarized yourself with his work by asking a question or two, and let the questions show your knowledge and competence. One Chicago veteran editor suggests finding out whatever you can about the writer before you do this. She also introduces herself, telling the author how long she's worked as an editor and what other books she's edited.

If you're lucky, you will be able to express sincere enthusiasm about the project. Tell the writer your proposed editing schedule and give him whatever contact information you want him to have. (Think twice about the cell phone number—although I've given mine several times and never regretted it.) Ask if he prefers to be contacted by e-mail or phone, and whether he minds your asking questions occasionally while you're reading, rather than all at once at the end. Once you've written this sort of letter a few times in your own words, you'll have a template for introductory letters that you can tailor to each new author.

Dear Mr. Writer:

[Introductory blah-blah]

Right away, I have a question for you. I notice you consistently cap Impressionism, but otherwise I don't see a clear system in your casing of art styles and movements. Baroque, classic, romantic, cubist, modern (plus their -ists and -isms) appear both ways throughout. Chicago style is to lowercase, so before I meddle, please let me know whether I should, and if so, your preferences.

Asking questions like this at the beginning will help give the writer confidence that you will pay attention to detail as you whip his stuff into shape. (This is carefulness.) It will reassure him that you'll make no sudden moves without his knowledge. (Transparency.) And it will demonstrate your willingness to listen and negotiate. (Flexibility.) But several additional benefits may result from your early queries. From a writer's response, you might gain important information about his attitudes and preferences. He'll make demands—or ask questions of his own. You'll see right away whether he has a relaxed or vigilant response toward someone whose red pen is poised over his text. You'll note how prompt he is in getting back to you, and whether he is curt, or long-winded, or funny. And at the very least, you'll save yourself work later searching for every mention of baroque, classic, romantic, cubist, modern (plus their -ists and -isms) in order to reinstate the meticulous system of casing the writer had checked and rechecked before submitting his manuscript, all of which you decided to lowercase without asking. (In the case of the capped art movements, I was so surprised by a famous writer's willingness to leave everything to me, I wrote back impulsively, "I was actually half hoping you'd be pompous and dictatorial and solve the problem by insisting on one way or another." He replied, "I'm sorry to have missed an opportunity to be pompous and dictatorial.")

If you are a freelancer whose role will end after you finish negotiating the editing with the author, your reassurances to a writer at this point may be limited to showing your willingness to view the editing as provisional and to discuss any issues that arise. If you are an in-house editor who will see the project through production, explain that from here on, you'll be ready to help with any request. If a writer replies that he wants his favorite aunt to rewrite his contract and his seven-year-old to supply the illustrations, write back that, wow, you aren't sure it can happen, but you'll get right on it. Then do your part to pass along his requests—as sincerely as you can—to the people who will tell him no.

SIX HABITS TO CULTIVATE—NOW

When you're ready to begin editing, stop. The start of a new manuscript is a heady moment. So far, so good—you haven't even had a chance to do harm. The writer has confidence in you. This is the time to remind yourself of six good habits that will prolong the honeymoon, or that at least will make damage control easier if disaster strikes anyway.

1. *Ask first, and ask nicely.* We've already agreed on some benefits of asking questions before you begin tinkering with a manuscript: they showcase your capability; they can save you work later; and the writer's answers give you clues to his personality and preferences. But in managing your relationship with a writer, questions serve another important purpose: they can foster a collaborative environment rather than an adversarial one. For this reason, it's good to frame your questions positively rather than negatively, even when you can hardly believe what you're seeing in the manuscript. Resist writing little passive-aggressive hints that the writer is a lazy moron or that his manuscript isn't up to your standards. ("Your style seems to change in every paragraph. I'm sure you know what you're doing—I'm so sorry I can't figure out your system. Would you mind explaining?") And I won't even mention the ass-covering benefits of asking first. (We'll get to that later.)

2. *Don't sneak (much).* If you're editing electronically, you'll probably use a feature called "tracking," or "redlining," that shows your changes in a way that keeps the original visible at the same time. For instance, if you insert text, it might appear underlined, <u>like this</u>; when you delete text, it will have a line through it, ~~like this~~. Because you can turn the tracking feature on and off at will, you will have the option of altering the text "silently," that is, with the feature turned off.

Some types of uncontroversial changes are not easy to display visually through tracking (such as eliminating double and triple spaces accidentally typed between words), so it makes sense to make them silently. You want your printout of the redlined manuscript to be as readable as possible. Other kinds of tracked changes, like the removal of hyphens, can be visually‐_confusing (see what I mean?). You could just change them—what the heck—and not say anything. But it's better to note such changes the first time ("-ly adverbs unhyphenated silently hereafter"). Keep a list of the types of silent changes you make and include it with the edited manuscript.[1] In your cover letter, offer to discuss any changes the writer finds alarming.

3. Eliminate surprises. If you steer clear of stealth-editing, you eliminate one type of unpleasant surprise for your author, but without adequate warning, other shockers can arise, unrelated to the content of your editing. You might send him the manuscript just as he's leaving for two weeks of incommunicado research for a cover story on gorilla tracking in Central African Republic. Or you might discover that a book author has been planning all along to add a few illustrations after he sees page proofs. Here is actual, recent e-mail correspondence between one of my colleagues and a writer who was surprised to learn that he was responsible for indexing his book:

> **AU** / What index? Haven't I sent it already?
>
> **ED** / You sent a list of entries, but you need to add the page numbers—and in the proper format, as I mentioned. You'll have to take a pass through the pages to find the page numbers. This is not generated automatically, unfortunately.
>
> **AU** / This must be a mistake. Why can't it be done automatically? You guys have the electronic files, so why should it be done manually and by me?

1. Good candidates include serial commas, hyphens deleted after prefixes, and hyphens changed to en dashes in inclusive numbers. I like to note in my cover letter that such changes are made per *CMOS* and a particular dictionary.

Fortunately for you, all of these things have happened to me, so they needn't happen to you. When you first make contact with a writer, list all the deadlines you know, and ask about travel or teaching plans that could cause problems. (If you're editing news copy, your deadline issues will be very different, and your writers will already understand them.) Confirm whether the writer will be proofreading or making an index and mention that if he plans to hire a freelancer, you can help find one—if you have a few weeks' notice. (It doesn't hurt to hammer it in a bit: "Freelancers tend to be booked up in advance, so please let me know in plenty of time.") When you send the edited manuscript, make it clear that it's the writer's last chance to make major changes.

4. *Check in.* As the project progresses, take other opportunities to remind the writer of impending transactions. E-mail is a perfect tool for this. ("Hello—just checking in. Have you had a chance to look at the editing? Is everything clear?" "Hello—just wanted to let you know I expect page proofs in a couple of weeks, and to confirm that you're ready to read them. Is 50 Knoll Drive where I should send them? I'll be giving you until July 17 to get them back to me. I hope this is good timing—please let me know if you foresee any problems.")

Something I learned the hard way is that authors sometimes leave your package unopened until they're ready to work on it, so you can't rely on a cover letter to communicate the deadline. I once e-mailed to nudge a translator who was a bit late returning page proofs, and she replied, "When are they due? I haven't opened them yet." For this reason, it's good to reiterate the deadlines in an e-mail or phone call right after you receive notice from FedEx that the package was delivered (I make it a habit to request this notice), and while you're at it, ask the writer whether the package has arrived. Just because someone at CyberWidgets International signed for it, doesn't mean it's not languishing in a corner of the mailroom.

Make sure your cover letters are clear about the writer's tasks, and take the opportunity to prepare him for the next steps. When a writer is reviewing your editing, for instance, it's important for him to know whether or not this is his last chance to make changes. Your cover-letter template should stress this. ("Finally, this is the time to make all your last corrections. At page-proof stage, changes can be expensive and even risky, since they sometimes cause additional errors, and you will not have a chance to proof the revisions." I long ago saw a letter that a former boss and mentor wrote to an author adding something like "Sorry to sound bossy—it just seems a good idea to prevent disaster if possible." I've copied it all these years.)

5. *Keep it professional.* There are bound to be times when you and a writer click so well that your working relationship edges toward friendship, and I'm not going to tell you to slam the door on that. But I will point out that being the writer's advocate is not the same as being his buddy. As long as you are handling his manuscript, your first loyalty is going to be to the reader, and there will be times when a little professional distance will make this easier. It's not unheard of for a writer to develop, let's say, personal-boundaries issues with an editor: one author sent a colleague of mine a photo of himself wearing a fake (she hopes) tattoo of a heart with her name in it. What's more, as another colleague reminded me, "If you're extra nice, they take advantage of you."

In this vein, professionalism begins the first time you write to "Dear Mr. Surname," not to "Dear Bob." Although some of the young people I talk to think this courtesy has gone the way of the dinosaurs, the fact is that the dinosaurs are usually calling the shots, and if you annoy one, it's your problem. If Mr. Surname writes back "Yours, Bob," then fine. (One of my colleagues was charmed by a courtly southern author who, after months of intense collaboration from a distance, wrote, "I am now ready to call you Leah, if you would call me Beauregard.")

We'll talk more about e-mail management later, but in the context of maintaining a professional demeanor, make it an unbreakable rule (even at the risk of blowing your reputation as a subversive) to reply promptly to a writer's query whether you know the answer or not. It takes only a few seconds to reassure her that you're listening. ("Dear Beth: I don't know, but I'll find out and let you know asap.") Apologize freely for lapses or delays, but don't explain them in more than vague terms. Complain to your dog that you got slammed with three deadlines more pressing than Beth's. To Beth, you're simply sorry about the delay. Never whine. At the office, anyway.

Let me expand on that last point: it's rarely a good idea to explain more than is absolutely necessary. That's counterintuitive, because our first impulse is to appease, to defend ourselves, to receive permission, to *explain*. But when you mention specifics, you provide ammunition for rebuttal on each point. Better to be firm but vague. By giving you the following personal example, I'm risking complete humiliation. But (1) I want to save you from making similar mistakes, and (2) I want you to know that I don't pretend for a minute to live the life of a perfect, together, blissed-out editor. Just the opposite: I mess up *all the time*. It's how I know things. So here's an e-mail I drafted more recently than I'm happy to admit. The note is to the organizer of a "webinar" who kept increasing her demands on my time until I felt I could no longer participate. (I should have known from the minute I read the word "webinar" that nothing good could come of it.)

> "BEFORE" VERSION: Gertrude, I'm very sorry, but I fear that I'm not a good fit for your webinar. I had a hunch from the beginning that I was too clueless about the corporate setting to meet your expectations, and this confirms it. You assumed I'd have slides and never even thought to mention it, whereas it wouldn't have occurred to me in a million years. I've never made a slide in my life and have no idea how slides could possibly enhance my remarks.
>
> You seem to be expecting a presentation of some kind, and I simply don't have the time or motivation to provide one. I'm so sorry—I agreed as a courtesy to make a few remarks about the *Manual of Style* for your webinar, and I tried to stress that I wouldn't have more than a few minutes of thoughts about the importance of editing to a style. Quite frankly, I have to keep in mind that the U of C Press isn't invested in your product and you aren't paying for my time, and it would simply be wrong for me to spend more than a few minutes preparing for the event. I don't even have that kind of time on top of my responsibilities here.

I'm afraid I have to bow out. Again, my sincere apologies for the misunderstanding. I hope the event goes well.

And here's the note I actually sent, after my boss read the drafted e-mail, appeared at my door, and frowned. "Don't explain," she said. Oops—right.

"AFTER" VERSION: Gertrude, I'm very sorry, but I'm afraid my schedule and responsibilities are going to force me to withdraw from your webinar. I hope this news comes in time for you to recruit another speaker. I'm sorry for any inconvenience. I wish you all the best.

6. Say "Yes." One of the great things—perhaps the only great thing—about being low on the totem pole of publishing power is that there is a lot you don't get to decide, which means that you also don't have to say no. Instead, you can say, "I'll ask." There are many times, however, when you do have to decide, and your inclination will be to say no. I always have that impulse when a writer wants to reinstate something I consider ungrammatical. But still, when a writer asks something of you, at least consider accommodating the request.

A British translator of a French book recently stetted my change of "that of him who seeks" to "that of he who seeks."[2] In response, I asked for clarification and was ready to listen. ("On p. 142, I wanted to change 'that of him who seeks' to 'that of he who seeks,' and you nixed it. Are you sure? I don't see that the French is ungrammatical.") The translator replied with an explanation of the grammar as he'd learned it at school, and how he thought it might be an American vs. British thing. Although I admit that my first reaction was "No way," I resisted the thought, reached for *Fowler's*, and began considering whether to allow the Briticism if he was right. Fowler backed me up, and the writer ceded the point. ("P.S.," he wrote affably, "Should we form a Pedants

2. *Stet* is Latin for "let it stand." It's what an author will write next to your editing if he wants the original reinstated. When this writer stetted my change, he was rejecting it.

Anonymous chapter?") I believe my open attitude made it easier for us to negotiate and reach an amicable conclusion on this point and others.[3]

EVERYBODY WINS

So far this is a pretty rosy picture. You've got your act together, the writer is jazzed to receive great editing from your capable hands, and all involved will get what they want: the reader will get a terrific read; the writer will win critical praise and royalties; and the publisher will rake in prestige and profits. You, in your quiet, anonymous way, will have the reward of a job well done and pride in contributing to the world's store of good literature.

But maybe you're thinking, "Easy for her to say," and wondering exactly how you're supposed to communicate carefulness, transparency, and flexibility to your author; how you're supposed to maintain all those habits when you're elbow-deep in a project. (Not to mention how you manage when you have the Manuscript from Hell.) So in the next chapter, let's take a closer look.

A / Although the sign was incorrect, I'm not sure you should annoy the person who provides the enchiladas.

---

3. The fact that my grammar was wrong is another story altogether.

CHAPTER THREE

Working for the Reader, through the Writer

CAREFULNESS, TRANSPARENCY, FLEXIBILITY

Q / Dear *CMOS* Editors: I once had an editing professor tell me, "Read through your style guides a few times. You won't remember every rule that's in there, but hopefully when you see something peculiar, a bell will go off in your head and you can look it up." Her advice has worked like a charm with the AP guide (a mere 400 pages). Problem is, *CMOS* is a pretty hefty manual to read through a few times start to finish! Can you SuperEditors offer a little advice on memorizing *CMOS* enough to get those little bells to go off in my head?

In chapter 2, I suggested that carefulness, transparency, and flexibility are the three paths to editing enlightenment. Let's take a closer look at how each of these can benefit both ourselves and our writers.

CAREFULNESS

Being careful while editing is a worthless gesture if you don't know what you're doing. A young editor I once supervised was extravagantly careful in inserting about a thousand commas to separate author and date in parenthetical source citations (e.g., Edwards, 1981). If he had taken that much care in studying *CMOS*, he would have known that Chicago style omits the comma. (If he had known even a little bit more, he would have decided to leave it alone regardless of Chicago style.)

The point is, when I talk about carefulness, I am actually talking about knowledge. If you don't know the current trends and rules of style and grammar, you won't be aware of all the little things that might or might not need attention in a manuscript. You can be the most meticulous person in the world as you start reading, but if you are ignorant of the issues, you will happily read past all the infelicities that should set off alarms. So the first step toward carefulness is to study your style manual. If it's a chunky doorstop like *CMOS*, it might be a gradual process, but keep your guide handy and make a habit of referring to it.[1] If a specific guide is not required for your work, pick one that appeals to you. And if you are new to editing, remember your mantra: "First do no harm."

A trove of knowledge, don't forget, exists in your author. She may be clueless about the style you are following, but she has two kinds of expertise that you may not: she knows her subject, and she knows the knowledge level of the reader she's writing for. In most editing

---

1. Here's some concrete advice for learning a style manual, in reply to a reader who wrote to ask whether there was a tutorial program for studying *CMOS*:

A / *"CMOS" for Dummies?* Not that I know of, although it wouldn't surprise me. But try not to be intimidated. Unless you're a technical writer, you can ignore some of the chapters and use them only for occasional reference. The goal is to know what's in the book and how to find it, not to memorize it. Start by skimming the chapter on manuscript preparation and editing, and if it applies to the work you're doing, read it more intently. Then look through the chapters on punctuation and spelling (read the detailed chapter tables of contents first). Again, the important thing is to educate yourself on the issues, not necessarily all the various solutions. Scan through the chapter on names and terms, so you'll know when you need to use it. (You will surely linger over "Titles of Works.") Read the introduction to the chapter on numbers, and if it holds your interest, keep reading. Look at the overall book TOC and all the chapter TOCs to see what issues apply to your own work. When you're feeling strong, tackle the chapters on documentation—where the real copy editors hang out. After that, just dip in when you encounter things you need to know. To some, the book's a page-turner—you may find yourself browsing, especially if you have the online edition.

projects, there will be issues you should leave to the writer, and doing so doesn't hurt your credibility. It would hurt your credibility to pretend you are fluent in Yorùbá. But don't just shove everything into her lap. ("Please remember that no one here will check the Yorùbá.") Do your part. Pay close attention and figure out whether the writer has been careful or not, and prod her if necessary. ("Please check all the Yorùbá. There are variations in the diacritics and in the way words are combined in otherwise identical phrases. These may be intentional, but I have no way to tell: *orí kí, oríkí, òrí kì,* or *oríkì*? There is also variation in upper- and lowercasing of terms. Perhaps you could answer my questions in your glossary first, and once the glossary is the way you want it, check terms against it as you read. I'm enclosing my style sheet for reference.")

Although we must credit the writer's knowledge of her field and her audience, don't assume she's up on every subtlety of grammar and style and will immediately recognize the wisdom of your corrections. If you make changes you think the writer might reject out of ignorance, especially if it's something you changed throughout a manuscript, explain why at the first instance. ("Chicago lowercases 'the board,' but uppercases 'Board of Trade,' hereafter silently.") Sometimes in my cover letter, I prepare a writer up front for my editing of a pervasive problem:

> When I query your choice or spelling of a word, it's often because I can't find support for it in a dictionary. In the case of technical jargon, just write "stet" if you like. But if you think other readers might also be confused, consider glossing the term. I'd like to clue in the uninitiated if possible, but I don't mean to annoy the cognoscenti. It's your call.

In this way, I try to demonstrate care and attention. At the same time, I identify an editing issue and express an informed preference, but defer to the writer's knowledge of the subject or her reading audience as the deciding factor.

Of course, you don't want to condescend or explain the obvious.

Explanations should be used sparingly—it's tedious for a writer to have to read endless justifications of the editing. That will only show your insecurities.

Finally, in addition to using your knowledge of style and grammar and the writer's knowledge of her field and her audience, use your own experience as a reader to inform your work as an editor, and don't hesitate to reference it in your explanations and queries. You've spent your whole life reading newspapers, magazines, books, and websites, noticing their ambiguities and lapses of logic. You've often wished you could ask the writer to elaborate or rephrase for clarity. This is your chance. Explain briefly why your more subtle changes are not gratuitous ("[*because you haven't introduced Stanpole yet*]" or "[*I stumbled here, taking 'picture' as a verb*]"). Use your own experience to suggest changes that will help the generalist reader, if it's appropriate.

TRANSPARENCY: THE SEE-THROUGH DOCUMENT

Since we've already seen many examples of how one edits transparently, I can be brief here. We let the writer know ahead of time what we're going to do, and we ask questions before we meddle in murky areas. We mark the manuscript clearly as we go, using the tracking feature of our word processors as well as written explanations of our decisions. And we summarize our decisions in a letter of editorial notes or a style sheet that we send with the edited manuscript. Transparency happens before, during, and after; and at all three stages, it invites the participation of the writer. Indeed, the purpose of transparency is to involve the writer in a collaboration, rather than work on your own and present the edited manuscript as a fait accompli.

Many copy editors, especially freelancers, may not have the opportunity to talk or e-mail with a writer directly during the work on her manuscript. Instead, you work through an intermediary. But that doesn't mean you get to exclude the writer from your process. Although you may have to make unilateral decisions for the sake of forging ahead, you can observe the same habits of care, transparency, and flexibility as you work. Whether it's your project editor, your boss, or the commissioning agent, there is usually someone who has requested your services and who will serve as a surrogate for the writer, either by helping you with important decisions or by asking the writer for you. If you eventually get the edited manuscript back from the writer for the cleanup stage, you will read her responses and copyedit any additions and corrections. If you are careful, transparent, and flexible as you work, the odds are better that the writer will be receptive to your editing, and you will have fewer loose ends to negotiate at that stage.

FLEXIBILITY: A STYLE IS JUST A STYLE

Of the three virtues I'm touting, flexibility is perhaps the most difficult for a copy editor to embrace. Carefulness almost goes without saying. By nature we are meticulous—probably you are insulted that I would even bother to mention the need for care in editing. And transparency is easier than ever to manage, with the use of redlining software. But I know from reading the Q&A mail over the years that when it comes to our editing decisions, it can be very, very difficult to be "flexible," when that seems to mean sacrificing everything we believe in. When we know a rule and have taken pains to impose it consistently throughout a document only to meet with the writer's resistance, our instinct is to go down fighting. It's a matter of honor. Of professional pride. And maybe even, just a little bit, of power. "My author insists on . . ." is one of the most frequent openers to Q&A readers' style questions. The very wording tells me that you are locked in a battle of wills. And by god, we have our standards.

There are several reasons I'd like you to reconsider this kind of inflexibility, and none of them involves the loss of virtue. For starters, by far the majority of the issues in queries to the Q&A are issues of style, rather than of grammar or documentation. A huge number of you write to *CMOS* for confirmation that a particular style rule is "correct":

My author caps the word "board" in sentences like "The board voted unanimously." Please confirm that this is incorrect.

· · ·

I want to delete the space after a colon in journal citations, per *CMOS* 17.169 (e.g., *Social Networks* 14:213–29), but my author disagrees. Can you please back me up on the correct style?

· · ·

I just got a manuscript back from an author who stetted every hyphen that I had deleted from words with prefixes (post-industrial, pre-war, etc.). I know it's correct to close them up, but his dictionary shows them with hyphens. I'm completely confused. Has this rule changed?

What these questions suggest is that copy editors fail to understand that style rules (which pertain to punctuation, capitalization, hyphenation, preferred spellings, and conventions for citing sources, among other things) are often by nature arbitrary and changeable. In comparison, grammar rules are more strict and less negotiable. Although grammar also evolves, its evolution is slower and more strongly resisted.

The inability to identify the difference between negotiable matters of style and nonnegotiable matters of standard English is perhaps the most common cause of grief among the writers to the Q&A. Not only are there many different and competing sets of style rules (*The Chicago Manual of Style* is only one), but they are different for a reason. Style rules serve purposes that aren't necessarily applicable to every kind of writing. For instance, the Associated Press (AP) style used by newspapers is based on selling newspapers to the masses. It promotes vocabulary accessible to readers of varying educational backgrounds. It avoids politically charged language, striving for a neutral and unbiased tone. (Minimizing word count must be another goal for newspapers: have you noticed their avoidance of "that" even when it's needed? "They maintained the house for years was a haven for crackheads." It drives me crazy.)

The publishers of educational materials for children have similarly purposeful style guides. The most rigid ones include word lists for each grade level and limit the number of words in a sentence.

The style guidelines in *CMOS* have accumulated over the years according to their popularity and usefulness in scholarly writing. They change from one edition to the next when they are no longer helpful. In the last edition, we decided to give up on the "9 January 1930" style and write dates the way most Americans do: January 9, 1930. We put the *n* back in "2nd." In the edition before that, in a matter where style intrudes upon grammar, we flirted shamelessly with using "their" as a nonsexist pronoun in singular contexts: everyone should hold on to their hats. (We aren't proud of that little indiscretion. Even then, we relegated it to a footnote in small type.) We constantly argue over whether to kill off the en dash. And we have stated regularly, since the very first edition in 1906, that "rules and regulations such as these, in the nature of the case, cannot be endowed with the fixity of rock-ribbed law. They are meant for the average case, and must be applied with a certain degree of elasticity."

The point is, your style guide—or any given "rule" you learned in school—was created so you would do something the same way every time for the sake of consistency, for the reader's sake. It's less distracting that way. You learn style rules so you don't have to stop and ponder every time you, say, come to a number in the text: "Hmm. Here's a number. Shall I spell it out? Use numerals?" You know your chosen style by heart, so you just fly by with confidence. Style rules aren't used because they're "correct." They're used for your convenience in serving the reader.

Although there are certainly some style conventions that are just as ironclad as the most accepted grammar and syntax rules, on the whole style is far more negotiable than you might believe.[2] If a writer has a preference that you can tolerate, consider doing so. If there's a

---

2. If you are copyediting for a professional journal, newspaper, or magazine, you may have very little flexibility in the styling of citations and certain other editorial tasks. But then, your writer won't be allowed to object to these styles, either.

reason why that style is inappropriate for the document, make your arguments and perhaps the writer will see reason.

Flouting the rules of grammar creates an impression that the writer is incompetent or uneducated. Most writers are grateful when we correct their grammar. Style is different. Flexibility in imposing style and in many other matters, then, is one of the key tools to managing good relationships with your writers. By indicating that your editing will be open to discussion, you give a writer reassurance that will inform your relationship from the start. I would never compare working with writers to parenting (because that would simply be wrong), but every parent knows that laying down the law is not often the smartest strategy, whether you are negotiating with a toddler or a teen. In editing, as in life, I have found "We can discuss this" to be a reliably effective suggestion. Sometimes the other party thinks, "Oh, well, since I have a choice, I'll let it go," and sometimes, "Omigod—she wants to discuss this endlessly. I'd rather just let it go."

By now we have spent three chapters preparing for our work with a writer or the writer's surrogate. We've arranged our priorities and established cordial communications; we've internalized some good habits; we have "Carefulness, Transparency, and Flexibility" tastefully tattooed somewhere upon our persons, or at least upon our psyches; we're doing whatever we can to master and retain knowledge of our house style. We're ready for anything.

But are we? In the next chapter, let's start facing our worst fears.

A / Memorize *CMOS*? Sadly, no. Even we are capable of completely forgetting whole sections of it at a time. And I'm sure few of us have read at full brainpower the chapters on mathematics and tables rather than dip in when we need to know something specific. It's simply not efficient to read and reread *CMOS* when so much of it is needed infrequently, especially now that we can search it electronically. Just read as much as you can; don't try to memorize.

CHAPTER FOUR

When Things Get Tough

Q / Oh, English-language gurus, is it ever proper to put a question mark and an exclamation mark at the end of a sentence in formal writing? This author is giving me a fit with some of her overkill emphases, and now there is this sentence that has both marks at the end.

Although bad things can happen to good editors without the slightest warning, there are other times when we can feel it in our bones that trouble's ahead. Sometimes we sniff danger in the manuscript; sometimes we sense it in the writer. In any case, it will be useful to identify resources for coping under siege conditions and have them at the ready.

Over my entire career in editing, I don't think I've encountered more than half a dozen difficult authors. By "difficult," I mean a writer who simply does not want changes made to his manuscript and is not even prepared to discuss them. We know the stereotypes: The hotshot journalist jealous of every comma. The poet who claims that his misspellings and eccentric punctuation are inspired. Assistant professors writing a first book for tenure are notorious for their inflexibility, and understandably so: their futures are at stake. They take editing personally; red marks on their manuscripts are like little stab wounds. And then there are vain authors who quarrel when we lowercase their job titles, who want their photos plastered all over the piece or their names in larger type. And don't get me started on writers who don't know what they're talking about, writers who are your boss, writers who are former high school English teachers.

One freelance manuscript editor told me of a writer who rejected all of her editing because he wanted to be "deliberately obscure." Another story came to me of a historian who insisted that the dashes in his subject's handwritten notebooks were of seven different lengths that had to be differentiated in typesetting. I recently edited a philosopher who fussed that his entire argument would become nonsensical if the book design didn't include little ornaments (>>><<<) in the line spaces. Probably the most startling story I've heard was about a freelance copy editor for a women's magazine who discovered that a writer—a famous "domestic diva"—had plagiarized a recipe. The poor freelancer mysteriously died the very same night she invited the writer to a dinner party at her house . . .

But I don't mean to worry you. Statistically speaking, I believe that the number of copy editors murdered by their authors is fairly low. In my experience, in fact, the more published the writer, the more tolerant and even grateful he is for the copy editor's help. He already knows how much embarrassment we can save him, and he's often busy with other projects and glad to pass the baton at the end stages of this one. The exception, of course, is a published writer who's been burned before by bad editing. (What—like it doesn't happen?)

Our task, regardless, is not to analyze the writer's insecurities, but to provide the best end product possible for the reader. When you sense from your opening communications that a writer may be resistant to editing, crank up all the precautions we've already discussed in order to smooth the way.

CARE TO THE NTH

As always, our watchwords are carefulness, transparency, and flexibility. Faced with a nervous author, you will save yourself much grief if right from the start you limit your expectations and work accordingly. Be extremely conservative in your editing. Keep in mind that this writer may have a take on his readers that you don't necessarily understand. Long ago in my first editing job for a popular national magazine, one of my tasks was to copyedit the movie review column of Judith Crist. A veteran writer with a huge and zealous following, Crist took pride in producing columns that needed no editing. I had never heard of her or read her reviews, and in my ignorance of her quirky habits and favorite phrasings, I annoyed her right away. There was a reason the new kid got to "handle" Ms. Crist—and I found out very quickly what it was. Thereafter I pretty much left her writing alone and stuck to fact-checking, and even then I would query rather than change anything. The rare times I found a typo or factual error, she ceded the point graciously, and gradually I was permitted to make an occasional tweak in syntax or word choice. We ended up getting along well, and she sent me a charming letter of thanks when I eventually left that job.

As you take extra care to do no harm, keep track of everything you do in case you have to undo it later, and indicate your willingness to discuss your decisions. If early on you see that the manuscript needs heavy editing or a great deal of cutting and you fear the response, send a sample for the writer's approval. If the amount of editing is likely to frighten the writer, consider printing two versions: one with the tracking visible and a second, clean copy. When I do this, I stress my reassurances: the sample is for the purpose of deciding how to proceed; everything is negotiable. ("I suggest you read the clean copy first. If you haven't looked at the manuscript for a while, it will be fresh to you, and you'll be able to see whether the text reads smoothly and logically in spite of the cuts. Then please do look at the deleted material to see whether something critical must be restored.") If your editing and cutting have been judicious, the writer will likely recognize it and direct you to carry on. If he's appalled, you'll have to ask for detailed feedback and work from there. Either way, you may be able to salvage a good working relationship.

If you're sending the manuscript without having sent a sample first, take the precaution of explaining some of the editing issues in your cover letter and emphasize your willingness to discuss them. Name the style guide and dictionary you used as arbiters in questions of consistency. Anticipate and try to prevent the writer from simply writing "stet" everywhere. ("I rarely intruded unless there was a problem with grammar or syntax or consistency of style, so if you don't like my solution to a particular problem, it will be helpful if you can suggest an alternative, rather than merely writing 'stet.' And of course I'm always happy to explain the editing if the reason for it isn't obvious.")

One last thought about extra precautions: If your contact with the writer reveals him to be the demanding type, be careful not to promise anything you don't have the authority to promise. A managing editor I know told me horror stories of one book manuscript editor who, without checking first, let herself be pressured into accepting an entirely new chapter from an aggressive author, another who allowed an author to add new art, and another who agreed to weeks of delay. These are serious gaffes—substantive additions to a book project must be vetted by the acquiring editor and possibly even subjected to further peer review. Additional art can blow a budget and affect everything from the cost of the book to the choice of typesetter and the delivery date. Weeks of delay can sometimes be tolerated, but other times delay will ruin a project's marketing plan. Sometimes the writer is contractually bound to meet deadlines. It's essential that delays be communicated to the project editor so she can strategize with the rest of the team. Remember: when requests come in that will affect a project's cost or schedule, you don't always have to say no; you just have to be careful about saying yes.

EXAMINING YOUR MOTIVES

Perhaps I should pause here to point out that writers aren't the only ones with ego issues. Copy editors tend to be smart and educated, and you have mastered a body of arcane knowledge that you apply daily in your work. You take pains to make good decisions, and when a writer rejects your decisions, your first response might be to take it personally, as an insult. If a writer pens rude replies on the manuscript, it's natural to feel annoyed or even angry. Oh, yes—we've all seen them:

"I wrote it that way because I want it that way"; "No!!! Stet!!!"; "This is wrong—put it back." A longtime Chicago manuscript editor tells the story of an author who wrote on the manuscript, "No, don't make this change." A few pages later he wrote, "I told you not to make this change." By the end of the manuscript he was writing, "HOW MANY TIMES DO I HAVE TO TELL YOU, DON'T MAKE THIS CHANGE!"

It's natural to want to assert your authority and win the point. It's natural not to want to give in. But it simply doesn't do any good to let those feelings have their way. Better to develop whatever mind tricks you can to calm yourself in order to be objective about it: *I did my job. It's his byline, not mine. My colleagues will sympathize when I rail about this. This will make a great dinner-party story. Someday I'll write a book.*

I'm not suggesting that you let yourself be battered into submission when a writer is clearly wrong about something. My point is rather that when you decide to argue a point, it should be on the merits of that point, not because you feel you have something to prove. Likewise, don't let a writer's mistreatment of you color your opinion of his every decision. Even jerks can be right sometimes.[1]

The last thing you want to do is ruin the chances for a civil collaboration. You aren't infallible yourself—remind yourself that a haughty reply will do nothing to ease tension or reassure the writer.

DEALING WITH BULLIES

When a writer's response to your editing borders on the belligerent, you may have a bully on your hands. If the manuscript is riddled with stets, give in to the more harmless ones; that is, undo the editing that you did merely for the sake of eloquence rather than correctness.

---

1. One colleague admits that more than once when a book went to type with blemishes he was unable to remove because of the author's resistance, he revisited the author's acknowledgments section to take out his own name. It's the kind of glory we can do without.

You've done your job. After you look over the manuscript and accept everything you possibly can, you will have to write a follow-up letter or e-mail in order to resolve the remaining loose ends. Use tact. Include some positive reactions. Thank the writer for his promptness or attention to detail; apologize for anything boneheaded you did that caused trouble. ("I'm sorry I misunderstood your system for displaying win-loss statistics; I wish now I had asked you first. Thank you for sorting me out.") If you can, say that you think the manuscript is now in much better shape as a result of his second pass.

If there are places where the writer seems to have rejected your editing without understanding the problem, spell it out. ("My thinking was that readers—or worse, reviewers—might wrongly take your wording to be sexist in nature. Can you suggest some kind of tweak to avoid that?") If there are global issues that you consider nonnegotiable, register your intent to override his stets without inviting a debate on each one. ("I have restored many of the commas that you requested. In places where they separate complete sentences, however, we need semicolons or periods, lest we drive the readers crazy. If there is a particular one of these you feel strongly about, we can discuss it.")

Depending on the stage you're at in the editing and production process, you might drop an issue momentarily, but return to it in your next communication. ("About that preface: I think we should add a line to your introduction explaining why it's at the back of the book.") If he won't budge, you'll have to show more firmness and determination, but as long as you can, leave the writer some room to make the decisions himself. ("Hello—just thought I'd let you know that I'm ready to submit the manuscript to production as soon as we resolve the preface issue. Any more thoughts on that?")

I have found that self-deprecation and humor have their place in dealing with difficult authors, but unless you are very sure how your idea of humor will be received, it might be better to resist.[2] Some

---

2. In my experience, most writers, like most people, have a funny bone, even if you wouldn't guess it from their prose. Most memorably, I encountered these lines in a book whose author was not only *not* difficult, but had a laugh with me when I gently pointed out

authors respond well to gentle teasing about their foibles, perhaps enjoying the self-image of writer as creative genius. ("Your abbreviations in this section were—forgive me—eccentric. I hope you don't mind that I swept through and standardized them.")

Be especially cautious when you are tempted to use humor as an antidote to bad news. Recently I wrote to tell an author who had requested three changes very late in the publication process that the designer, production manager, and I had decided we could make only two of them. In my e-mail to her, I breezily promised that we would make the third correction at the time of the first reprinting and went on to tell her about something funny that had happened to me since our last communication. I thought I knew the woman well enough, having worked on this project with her for over two years. Not only was she incensed that we wouldn't make the third correction, but she copied several people in on her reply to me—which included the goofy story I'd sent her. In that case my misjudgment not only affected my relationship with the author; it also embarrassed me in front of my colleagues. (As for her forwarding of my note, that's an issue I'll visit later when I talk about e-mail management.)

PICKING YOUR BATTLES

Since we've already agreed that there's no room for power-tripping as a copy editor, it stands to reason that there are going to be times when it's expedient to back down. Every editor feels strongly about certain issues, but it's good to reexamine the reasons behind those feelings when they get in the way of progress. Ask yourself whether you're pushing a rule because it's a rule, or because it serves the text

---

a problem passage (indeed, judging from his placement of the ellipsis, I suspected that a wicked sense of humor was at work when he wrote it in the first place):

> One of the more elaborate means of straightening the spine involved a metal halo attached to the skull with four screws and to the body cast with four vertical bars. One patient remembers that once the cast hardened, "every day a young resident would come by and . . . screw" her to straighten the cast and her spine.

and the reader in this case. Rules tend to become codified because they serve well in most instances, but sometimes they're just rules because our elementary school teacher made believers of us. The fixation that copy editors have for "correctness" is unbounded, as the mail to the Q&A attests.

Which is correct: "Find out who is the head of your division" or "Find out who the head of your division is"?

. . .

Can we start sentences with *because*? I have grown up learning the slogan "We cannot start a sentence with *because*, because *because* is a conjunction."

. . .

I have come across a construction that I am not used to at work: "We are focused against." I had been accustomed to saying "focused on." Can you please tell me which of these is correct?

. . .

Hi—just want to know which is correct: The goal of the course is to teach you in a *simple* way or *simpler* way.

When did we get the idea that English is so rigid a language that there is only one correct way to say something? Or the idea that consistency is mandatory or even desirable down to the minutest level of expression? My letters demonstrate a mania for correctness and consistency that, if applied universally, would turn every piece of writing into the same drab, expressionless, and mechanical style of prose.

Which is correct: "I have always hated sushi" or "I always have hated sushi"?

. . .

Should there always be a comma before the word *but*?

. . .

What's the rule for numbers: "The crowd was estimated at 2,000" or "The crowd was estimated at two thousand"?

. . .

Is there always a comma after "including"?

Of course there are many, many rules that are either so sensible or so universally accepted that they should be observed in the interests of giving readers prose that doesn't distract from the content of the document. Grammar rules and standards for citing evidence are the least flexible in this regard—but even then, there is room for opinion and debate. Different levels of formality in writing allow for variance as well—it would simply be wrong to robotically remove all split infinitives or all use of the passive from a piece of writing without considering whether the change would affect the writer's tone of voice or the emphasis intended in each instance.[3]

In each of the questions I quoted above, we see that the asker is tormented by the notion that there's an important rule at play and is trying to prove it, taking valuable time away from her work to research an issue that's not worth the time. Multiply this by the dozens—hundreds?—of such issues presented by a typical manuscript, and you have a stressed and inefficient worker.

What's more, when an editor becomes hung up on personal bugaboos like these, it can affect the actual editing in two negative ways beyond slowing it down. First, in your zeal to ferret out every last "which" and change it to "that," you are likely to overlook potentially more serious problems. You may have noticed this phenomenon yourself: often it seems that the more tinkering you do on a manuscript, the more errors remain. The writer will point out an error that you missed while editing, and you can hardly believe it got by you. Then you notice that in the preceding sentence, you had twice

3. I like Arthur Plotnik's point: "A little Strunk and White is a dangerous thing. Some editors are driven by a cursory reading of *The Elements of Style* to change such sentences as 'the outcry was heard round the world' to 'everyone in the world heard the outcry.'" Arthur Plotnik, *The Elements of Editing: A Modern Guide for Editors and Journalists* (New York: Collier/Macmillan, 1982), 3–4.

changed "due to" to "because of." Flush from that victory, you must have sailed right past the dangling participle.

Second, in covering the page with unnecessary and counterproductive little edits, you will alienate the writer and demonstrate the shallowness of your editorial judgment. Only the most thick-skinned of authors will fail to be irritated. And when a writer begins to believe that his editor is incompetent, his natural response is to start putting things back the way they were. All of a sudden you're adversaries—and all of the good work you did on his manuscript becomes a baby in the bathwater.

Which brings us back to the issue of knowing your stuff. When was the last time you looked at a recently published book on grammar and usage, rather than the one you used in school?[4] When you're deciding to go to the mat over your favorite authorial transgressions, reconsider. Can you find justification in more than one respected source? (Mrs. Hangstrup's 1980 lecture on not ending sentences with prepositions doesn't count.)

APPEALING TO AUTHORITY

You aren't alone, you know. When you find yourself debating an issue with a writer (or better yet, before it comes to that), use the tools at your elbow. During your work on the manuscript, justify editing decisions that you sense will mystify or annoy the writer, especially if you can tell from the writer's habits that your editing might seem inconsistent to him. ("I'll hyphenate the adj. *middle-class*, but not the noun *middle class*, per *Webster's*"; or "Pope Benedict, but the pope, per

4. If you feel out of date in your knowledge of grammar issues, have a look at *The Cambridge Grammar of the English Language*, by Rodney D. Huddleston and Geoffrey K. Pullum (Cambridge: Cambridge University Press, 2002). The book takes a descriptivist (as opposed to a more conservative prescriptivist) approach that many editors regard as too lax to be helpful, but browsing through it may give you an appreciation for developments since you last studied grammar.

CMOS 8.29.")[5] Please don't do this more than very occasionally—you aren't being paid to document and defend your every move, and, paradoxically, you will damage your credibility if you feel compelled to do so, by seeming to lack confidence in your own knowledge and judgment. Instead, do it a couple of times near the beginning of a project and coast on the impression it gives: that you know what you're doing and you rely on authority. Once you show that you know your sources, it's understood; you needn't keep expressing them. ("I'll spell out numbers up to a hundred hereafter, with some exceptions for 'regional consistency.'") If you make a habit of enclosing a copy of your style sheet with the edited manuscript, you can save yourself many explanations.

If you find that your appeal to published sources still hasn't won the day, you can always turn to human resources. At the risk of sounding all lemons-into-lemonady, I'll revisit one of the advantages of the humble status of the copy editor: there is almost always someone we can turn to when we need help with an unreasonable writer. It's not something you want to do regularly. Supervising editors don't have time for high-maintenance copy editors and will tend to look elsewhere if your learning curve seems to depend entirely on them. But they are all used to occasional appeals for help, and it's part of their job to intervene on your behalf when necessary. (My first managing editor and mentor at Chicago, the great Margaret Mahan, was once so exasperated by an author who complained unreasonably about one of her manuscript editors that she told him he was full of shit—although, in hindsight, she does not recommend that approach.)

Finally, on certain issues, remember that you get the last word. True, the writer's name is in the byline, but it's not the author's right to offend or confuse the reader, defy the rules of standard English, fail to identify sources, or lower the standards of your institution. It's likely that his contract says something to the effect that the publisher is allowed to make final editorial decisions in nonsubstantive style

5. You can specify which *Webster's* in your cover letter.

matters. Still, don't sneak: it's not fair simply to arrange things your own way in the version you send to the typesetter without settling the matter with the writer. ("I've made all the corrections we agreed on, but I'm afraid that without a source or explanation for the Cheney quotation, I was forced to go with the paraphrased version we discussed.") Most authors won't sue.

A / In formal writing, we allow both a question mark and an exclamation mark only in the event that the author was being physically assaulted while writing. Otherwise, no.

CHAPTER FIVE

Dear Writers

Q / I have one editor who does not like the serial comma, in particular, and prefers to use fewer commas, in general; and another editor who keeps trying to put the edited-out commas back into the text. I am just the lowly author who is stuck negotiating between the two of them. Help!

A chapter for the author was not in the original plan for this book. Some copy editors might even feel that our secret and subversive club won't seem authentic without a "No Writers Allowed" sign tacked up on the tree house. But while I was working on the book, I was surprised more than once when writer friends said they wanted to read it. I assured them that what they wanted to read was a book written by acquiring editors or developmental editors—not manuscript editors.[1] And they told me I was wrong.

Writers, understandably, have mixed feelings about having their work copyedited, and they are curious and sometimes nervous about

---

1. Acquiring editors are the ones who scout out manuscripts and buy them for a publisher. They generally specialize in one or more subjects or types of literature. If a project isn't yet in publishable form, an acquisitions editor might help the writer develop it, either before or after it's under contract. Or he might turn it over to a developmental editor, who will analyze the project and work with the writer to pull it into publishable shape. Both types of editors might do some copyediting while they're at it, but it's likely to be random and (forgive me) inconsistent. They assume a copy editor will go over it later.

the process. They would like to know what they can do to prepare for it and what to do if they disagree with the changes. And since one of the main points of this book is to welcome writers into our club (and since, as a writer, I'm about to experience being on the other side of the desk myself), it seems right to think about things from the author's point of view.

ACTS OF SUBMISSION

Occasionally a writer handing in work will suggest skipping the copy-editing stage, offering assurance that the manuscript has been read several times. Some of my authors have noted that they even paid for freelance editing before submitting their manuscripts. Although it is true that some manuscripts are in excellent shape, in my experience the likelihood that a given project will need no editing bears little relation to the number of times it has been vetted by colleagues, employees, or children of the writer. I would go further and venture that if I were to pluck any published book or magazine article from the library shelf and surreptitiously have it scanned into manuscript form for editing, most copy editors would still find a fair bit to meddle with.

How can this be?

First, the habits and standards and style manuals of publishers vary. Even more to the point, the preferences and knowledge of manuscript editors vary. A lot. Comma choice alone leaves so much room for discretion that it would be nearly impossible for two editors working independently to punctuate a manuscript of some length in the same way. A certain amount of editing is optional and subjective. What one editor considers acceptable is incorrect to another. One reads with his eyes, another with her ears, and they edit accordingly. Some concentrate on logic and flow; some are sticklers for grammar; and some, like an indulgent mother with a sticky toddler, let everything but the most obvious and egregious messes slide by.

Even if all editors were of the same sensibility and training, editing is by nature multitasking, reading at several levels simultaneously—

in fact, it's common for editors to read their manuscripts twice, concentrating on big-picture issues in one reading, details in the other. Inevitably, we are distracted as we read by the issues that interest us the most, and inevitably we overlook or dismiss some matters as unworthy of attention.

My point is that a manuscript will never be edited the same way twice, and it will never be considered perfect, no matter how many times it's edited—probably not even by the last person who edited it. (An assigning editor at a famous children's magazine told me of her exasperation after one of her staff had copyedited the same text in three revisions and kept finding errors. "Stop looking for mistakes!" she yelled. "Think like an editor and just let it go!")

The second reason that a manuscript must undergo copyediting regardless of its state at submission is that it must be prepared for typesetting. Although a writer under contract is usually given guidelines for formatting and organizing her manuscript, it's the rare author who follows the guidelines closely enough to deliver a document ready for production. A good amount of the copy editor's time must be spent in removing pretty Word styles, redoing weirdly typed block quotations (the kind with tabs at the beginning of every line), and cleaning up whatever else the writer did while trying to be helpful in spite of the guidelines. (Writers are endlessly inventive—or ignorant—when it comes to word processing. Years ago a colleague showed me a book manuscript that consisted of 350 Microsoft Word documents; the author had started a new file each time he reached the bottom of a page.)

So when you submit a manuscript—even if your manuscript consists of previously published materials—be prepared for someone to find something that needs changing. And when you read somewhere that writers should try not to take editing "personally," realize that this is why. A certain amount of copyediting has very little to do with how great a writer you are.

If you work in a specialized area or have unconventional content in your manuscript, prepare to be edited by someone who is not an expert in that area—or a mind reader. If you're lucky, she will have experience editing related books or articles, but if she hasn't, she will welcome a page from you with explanations and preferences. (For example, "The term 'improvisative' should not be corrected to 'improvisational' or 'improvisatory'"; or "Please don't change the spellings of place-names; it's a political issue.")

In light of all this, is it worth the time and money to hire a copy editor in advance of submitting your work? That depends. On the one hand, if you feel that your writing is in pretty good shape, there's little point in paying someone to copyedit to a particular style only to have your publisher redo it to a different one. On the other hand, if your readers have been marking a lot of typos and writing "huh?" in the margins here and there, your manuscript might benefit from a pass specifically addressing those kinds of issues.

There are other good reasons to get professional help before submission. If you are submitting work that requires you to identify sources and you aren't confident that your notes and references are complete and conform to one of the commonly accepted styles (Chicago, AP, APA, etc.), a copy editor can put things right. If you are trying to break into a field of writing and your work is being done on speculation, small sloppinesses can land your work in the rejection pile. An editorial eye can tidy up the remaining flaws.

THE WAITING GAME

While your manuscript is in copyediting—for a day, a week, or sometimes months—it might be difficult for you to keep your hands off it. That's understandable, and it's not a terrible thing, but there are two reasons why it would be better if you could let it rest, for now. First, there's a chance that you'll merely be duplicating work that your editor is doing, and you'll only waste her time by asking her to check a list of typos that she's already corrected. And second, your work will benefit from your gaining a little distance on it. You'll get a chance soon enough to read the entire thing again when the editing is sent for your approval, and if you've been away from it thinking about other things, you'll return to it with a fresh eye.

It's possible that even if you're trying not to think about your manuscript, various corrections, additions, and little improvements will occur to you anyway. Just write them down so you can tend to them when it's your turn. You might be able to get a sense of whether your copy editor minds you e-mailing bits and pieces to her while she's working. I always appreciate having the information right away, so I can incorporate it while the style particular to that project is fully in my mind. Others don't want the distraction and would rather you make all your corrections later, at one time. Try to respect your editor's wishes.

Occasionally during the downtime, a writer finds that she's completely rethinking a major point—even to the extent of adding new text or an appendix. It's the author's responsibility to alert the copy editor of the new development the minute it becomes a real possibility. The copy editor can then decide whether the change in plan is serious enough to warrant running by the boss, the assigning editor, the acquiring editor. If the new section will need expert review, the publisher might want to rethink the schedule, and the copy editor might be asked to put the project aside until everything is resolved. The magazine article will run in a later issue; the book will deliver in the fall instead of in the spring.

Something you should never do once editing has begun is to make changes to the original e-files in the expectation that you can send them to the copy editor, who will somehow incorporate this new version into her work. I cannot stress enough how unreasonable this would be. (Note that nowhere else in this book have I italicized for emphasis as many words in a row.) By the time you send it, she will have spent hours cleaning and coding and making countless silent changes to your files. In your new version, perhaps you made a change here and there— maybe a dozen tweaks in all—but she will have to start editing from scratch, having no way to know what your changes were. (The nature of her electronic cleanup will make a "compare documents" operation nearly useless.) Of course, if I were that editor, and if I were feeling in control and professional, I would just suck it up and deal with the disaster. After all, it's your work. You're my second master, next to the reader. I want what you want.

But it's possible that I would be more human than that: it's possible that I would hate you and lose all interest in your project.

(Just so you know.)

WHAT? WHERE? WHEN?

While you were in the process of writing, you may have had the luxury of dawdling. Once your book or article is in copyediting, the schedule becomes a much more real and serious part of the process, and one that you will have little control over—other than to cause delays when the ball is in your court. Although most writers are eager for their work to appear and will do everything they can to expedite publication, a surprising number are more casual about deadlines and seem to think nothing of racking up significant delays in the return of edited manuscripts, page proofs, or indexes.

If you are writing for a periodical or any project with a short schedule, the deadlines will be pretty much set in stone; a writer who procrastinates may simply be ignored while her project is either jettisoned or taken over by someone else. So ask ahead of time when you will be expected to be available to vet the editing or look at proofs, and if anything comes up that you think might interfere with the schedule, give reasonable warning. If your editor knows in advance about schedule conflicts, she might be able to reshuffle things with typesetters and publicity contacts or move your work to another issue or season. Unexpected holdups will leave everyone in the lurch.

For longer-term projects like books, there are still good reasons to respect your publisher's schedule, and most of them directly benefit your project. Once a publisher makes a commitment to your book, every department, from editing and design to production and marketing, sets about creating the optimal conditions for its release. The schedule is a small miracle of coordination between departments, and a delay at any point can cause an equal delay in publication or, worse, will compound into disaster.

EDITING AS A GIFT, NOT AN INSULT

You know what it's like to come back to a hotel room in the afternoon and find that housekeeping has been there and everything is all fresh and put to rights? That's how a copy editor would like you to feel when you see the editing. If you can view extra-duty editing as the mint on the pillow, all the better. What we don't want is for you to feel insulted that we saw the need for cleaning.

If a manuscript editor has made a smart suggestion, brought clarity to a badly written passage, inspired you with a leading question, or pointed out a flaw in your argument, how are you going to react? I can guess your first thought: you will wish you had done it yourself. And almost every writer has been appalled at a boneheaded error that survived all the way to the copy editor. A magazine fact-checker told me of a celebrity puff piece in which the writer quoted an actor claiming to have hiked 5,723 miles straight up a mountain, and a profile in which another writer had absentmindedly typed the name of her tailor instead of the name of an actress's father. (The writer's claim ticket had been tacked on the bulletin board in front of her while she typed.) The fact-checker spent hours trying to verify the connection.

Your second reaction will be to resent someone else's having done it (and a mere copy editor at that), and your third impulse will be to wonder whether it's fair for you to accept what she has done and present it as your own.

Of course it's fair. That's our job. It's what we hope for. Nothing is more gratifying than for us to receive a manuscript back from a writer with the editing for the most part intact. One of the nicest responses I've ever had to my editing was in the form of an author's addition of a paragraph to the end of his novel. In my cover letter, I had mentioned my initial surprise and disappointment at the ending, and I explained why, although I added that, feelings aside, I knew it was the only sensible ending. The new paragraph addressed my feelings perfectly, without changing the facts of the ending. I couldn't have been more pleased.

We know that writers don't work in a vacuum, and that before your work reaches us, it's been improved at many stages by the encouragement and critiquing of others. You've done the most difficult part, gathering the research, organizing, thinking, getting the words onto the page, revising in response to criticism. You've made it easy for us to read the finished product and pick at the little rough spots.

Two ways you can continue to make things easy for your copy editor: (1) Respond at least minimally to every question or comment on the manuscript. Even if you decide that your original is correct, a little checkmark beside the query will tell the copy editor that you read and considered her remarks. (2) Submit lengthy or complex addenda in both hard copy and electronic form. That way your prose will be exactly the way you want it rather than however the copy editor deciphers your marginal scrawlings.[2]

And here's a plea straight from the collective heart of copy editors everywhere: Please take a few minutes to read through the cover letter or instructions enclosed with your manuscript or page proofs. And after you read them, *follow* them. We are continually astonished that grown-up professionals, many of whom have probably railed for years at their students for not reading directions, fail to observe the simple instructions for marking up edited copy or proofs. This can make a great deal of extra work for your editor. I myself just finished about eight hours (including five on a Sunday) of re-marking proofs for an author who wrote between the lines, failed to flag corrections in the margins, marked contradictory directions by using the wrong symbols—I could go on and on. I cleaned up the mess myself instead

---

2. Please note that I said "addenda," not "revisions." Revised text must never be submitted as retyping. If this idea is new to you, please go back and reread the paragraph that begins with all those italics in the section called "The Waiting Game."

of sending them back because I was getting ready to leave on vacation and the deadline was an important one.

Just because there's a cleaning crew doesn't mean you get to throw food on the floor.

"ILS ONT CHANGÉ MA CHANSON . . ."

If all goes well, you'll be happy with the editing of your manuscript. But what if you aren't? What if you start reading and right away you see that you've been terribly misunderstood? The copy editor has rewritten phrasings that are standard and necessary in your field. She's removed a numbering system that she didn't realize is based on a related work. Where you chose not to define terms, she's added glosses that your readers will find patronizing and juvenile. She's struck through all the personal names that you transliterated according to the linguistic system you're celebrated for inventing and replaced them with spellings she found at Wikipedia.

Don't panic. Keep reading, make notes, and keep an open mind. Everything that has been changed can be changed back, and you should assume that your editor will be willing to do so. Small matters of style are most likely to be negotiable. A researcher and copy editor at one national magazine told me that after John Updike complained about the house spelling of "kidnaped" and "kidnaping," the publisher changed the stylebook to Updike's preferred "kidnapped" and "kidnapping." Even if you aren't John Updike, you still might get what you want if you ask.

Look at an offending edit and figure out why the editor thought the text needed help. There will usually be something wrong that needs fixing: after all, if the editor misunderstood you, other readers may, too. If you don't like the editor's solution, figure out a better one and write it in. If you are convinced that the original wording is the way you want it, mark a row of dots under everything you want restored and write "stet" beside it. And unless you want to go another round on the issue with the editor, pencil in a brief explanation.

Although you might find yourself infuriated by clueless or incompetent editing, the second-worst thing you can do is explode in anger and rail at the copy editor. (The worst thing you can do is explode in anger and rail about her to her superiors.) Explain in the margins or in a cover letter why the editing was misguided. Although it might be difficult for you to rein in your exasperation, there's no point in humiliating and abusing the editor, and it will only make it more difficult to negotiate the editing.

Although you will likely find your copy editor willing to restore almost everything you insist upon, it's usual for there to be a few matters she will want to discuss further. If there were places where you simply wrote "stet" without addressing the problem in the writing that she was trying to fix, the problem will still be there. She may write back explaining the problem and asking you to find a way to fix it. You may be tempted to dismiss her perception of a problem as imaginary, but that would be a mistake. If one reader stumbles, others may, too, and you would do well to address the issue.

In the extreme circumstance that the normal process of negotiating does not induce your copy editor to undo her editing, you may have to go over her head with a complaint. Please consider this a last resort, after trying first to resolve things with the editor directly. In my department recently, an author complained about one of us to the acquiring editor, claiming that the editing was capricious and inconsistent and demanding a new copy editor. The acquiring editor was duly alarmed and promised to review the editing with our managing editor. As assistant managing editor, I witnessed this conversation and saw how readily the acquiring editor took the author's word. Review of the manuscript, however, showed that the author had been hasty to judge, probably because of his unfamiliarity with Chicago style. In not bothering to ask the copy editor about her method before complaining, he caused her some temporary humiliation, cost others the time needed to review the manuscript, and earned a reputation as a nuisance.

On the other hand, if you're happy with the editing, feel free to say so—to the copy editor herself, to her employers, or in the acknowledgments section of your article or book. Without face-to-face contact, we can't always guess how our authors really feel. Acknowledgment— or the lack of it—often surprises us. The experience described by a colleague may be typical: as often as not, a writer whose manuscript needed almost no work will praise him effusively, while an author of a book he sweated blood cleaning up will overlook him entirely.

Here's a former colleague's favorite compliment from a writer: "Without changing anything [you] changed everything for the better. Sleight of hand is the editor's best tool." Another colleague was publically praised in an author's acknowledgments for having the skill "to make her improvements in my text seem like what I was just on the verge of writing myself. But without her, I wouldn't have."

Goodness knows, copy editors aren't in it for the glory—but when we believe we've brought significant improvement to a project, it can make our day to learn that the author thinks so, too.

A / I'm afraid your intuition is correct that this is a matter of preference. So you have two editors, and they disagree? I'd say it's time for you to form a preference of your own and use it to divide and conquer.

PART TWO

WORKING WITH YOUR COLLEAGUES AND WITH YOURSELF

In my experience, most writers are competent and cooperative in their response to the kinds of problems copy editors grapple with every day. They appreciate our look at their work and are often apologetic when they see the kinds of housekeeping their manuscripts require.

No, the author is not the enemy. To find the most common causes of our angst and insomnia, we must look closer to home, at difficulties that have nothing to do with the ultimate reception of our work by the writer. In the second half of this book, I will turn to the subject of getting along with ourselves and others on the job. I will write about ways to meet our daily challenges and consider how we sometimes create difficulties for ourselves that we could avoid or remedy by shifting our attitudes and developing new habits. Some of my suggestions may cause grammar and style sticklers among you to reach for your smelling salts—but please hear me out. The rules I want you to break are not really rules; the standards I want you to lower are merely barriers to good and efficient editing.

Some years ago, a study appeared showing that the most stressful work conditions occur when the worker has a great deal of responsibility but very little power. (It's possible that I made that up; nonetheless, it's plausible.) Some of you might think that would include us—after all, we have the responsibilities, the deadlines, the tedium; the fear that errors will be complained about by authors, noticed by readers, trumpeted by reviewers. And there's the lack of power: we don't set deadlines; we don't set style. In the publishing world, our status is low, our income disproportionate to our education, our skills, and the value we bring to the written project.

If you are reading this book, it is possible that you are just such a stressed-out copy editor. You are an intelligent, sensitive, conscientious soul ready to buckle under the strain of too much work to finish perfectly in too little time. You stay up nights to meet deadlines; you work through weekends. You cry. And that is very wrong; there should be no crying in copyediting.

When you are under pressure to do work that is difficult for any reason, you need some coping strategies. That is what I will try to offer in the remaining chapters.

CHAPTER SIX

When Things Get Tough (the Sequel)

THE DANGEROUS MANUSCRIPT

Q / I am creating a style guide for a company that does not use the serial comma. For the sake of consistency, I am considering stating in the guide that the serial comma is not to be used at all (yikes!). My question is: Is it better to be consistent (and not use the serial comma at all) *or* to add in the serial comma ONLY when it is necessary to prevent ambiguity? I wish that I could just DEMAND the use of the serial comma at all times, but, alas, I am just a lowly intern.

Copy editors who work for corporations or publishers of technical or academic books are more likely to handle lengthy and complex manuscripts than those at magazines and newspapers, but a manuscript can be challenging in many different ways. It can be highly technical or theoretical. It can contain Swahili or Japanese, mathematical equations, complex graphs and tables, inscrutable figures, insider jargon, or hundreds of citations, none of which appear to be consistently styled. It can be badly written, or typed with exasperating word-processing techniques. It can just be long.

But to a copy editor, these are all in a day's work. We take the problems line by line, like quilter's stitches, and when we're doing well, we feel competent and in control. We keep track of our decisions on a style sheet; one page at a time, we establish order and coherence where it is lacking.

In my experience, a manuscript becomes "dangerous" in one of two ways. The first is when the tasks it requires seem mindless, that is, overwhelmingly tedious and repetitive; and the second is when the tasks are the opposite of mindless, that is, unusually complicated. In both cases, I worry about taking too much time over them, or doing them badly out of boredom or haste, or introducing errors through careless automation. Faced with a dangerous manuscript, we must do everything we can to prevent the disaster that's waiting to happen.

THE MINDLESS TASK

In a just world, copy editors would never be presented with mindless tasks. It's true that as word-processing tools have become more sophisticated, we can magically dispense with a great many such chores. The flip side, however, is that our writers deploy the same tools. Not only does this allow them to create electronic nightmares that we are left to sort out; it also gives them the idea that almost any problem they might impose can somehow be handled automatically. But we shouldn't be asked to renumber 389 figures and all of their corresponding call-outs and mentions in the text because the author didn't end up getting permission for figure 3. We shouldn't be asked to transpose the first and last names in a fifty-page list of corporate sponsors because the author typed them the wrong way around. We shouldn't be asked to embed footnotes electronically that the author provided in a separate file.

Nonetheless, we do face such chores, and I have three strategies for tackling them: automate, delegate, or reevaluate.

1. *Automate.* My first strategy for tackling a long, tedious chore is always to find a word-processing shortcut. If the task must be done, and if I believe it can be automated in some way, I will spend two hours trying to figure out how rather than one hour doing it by hand. At least that way I'll know how to do it the next time. I look in a manual, browse online, or as a last resort ask my "guy." (Everyone should have a guy—

who of course can be a gal. A guy is someone who knows everything, has endless patience, and is always available and responsive. To maintain good relations with your guy, you must be very careful to bother him only occasionally and only when all else fails. Although I have a fabulous guy, there's a sort of food chain of competence here; I believe that several people actually consider me to be their guy.)

If a task cannot be automated, and if it must be done, I will be blunt about my next strategy: I try to get out of it.

2. Delegate. If you are lucky enough to work where the submission guidelines for writers have some bite and the assigning or acquiring editors have some backbone, send the unruly manuscript back "upstairs," as we say at Chicago. It is the author's responsibility to see that his manuscript conforms to the basic house requirements. They might decide upstairs that an important author should be let off the hook, but if not, don't worry about his having to labor over his laptop for a few more hours—that's what hungry interns and grad students are for. If you are lucky enough to work for an office that employs assistants or interns (and if you are ruthless enough to exploit them), another ploy is to toss it their way—although my own rule of thumb is that if my time is too valuable for a particular chore, the same might well be true for an assistant's.

If you are an intern or assistant or hungry grad student—well, we thank you. Hang in there; your day will come.

If you are a freelancer, consider asking for help. Your employer or supervising editor might sympathize. She may very well feel that she is paying you to spend your time on more important tasks and agree to find someone else for the more clerical chores. In the boilerplate part of my cover letter to freelancers, I ask them not to take on any time-consuming mechanical task without checking with me first.

Some copy editors employ subcontractors for work that is tedious, specialized, or simply too much to do in the allotted time. This is a legitimate option if it's done with the knowledge of all involved. Your employer is paying you a given rate because she knows your work and values it accordingly. It's not right to turn in the work of less experienced workers and represent it as your own. But if you can define a chunk of the work to be done under your supervision and you accept responsibility for it, your employer might agree.

When you delegate—whether to a freelancer, an assistant, or the author—consider it a privilege, and don't abdicate your fundamental responsibility of oversight. Any time someone else handles electronic files for you, there is the possibility that new errors will end up costing you more trouble than you saved. I rarely let e-files out of my control once I've started working on them. The ideal time to get help is before you start editing, so you can check the corrections as you go. But if there's absolutely nobody waiting in the wings to do your dirty work for you, there is a last resort:

3. *Reevaluate.* If you find that you don't have what it takes to dump a hated task into someone else's lap, consider the possibility that your conscience is trying to tell you something. That is, is it possible that the task should not actually be done by anyone? Sometimes mindless tasks are necessitated by a poorly prepared manuscript, but other times we impose them on ourselves out of a misguided drive to perfect what does not need perfecting.

Any time you find yourself looking at a repetitive task that is going to add a significant amount of time to the editing of a manuscript and that cannot be automated, stop and think about it. Is the offending material actually incorrect, or is it simply not styled conventionally? Will it inconvenience or confuse the reader? Get a second opinion from a colleague. Ask your supervising editor if she thinks it's worth your time. And if finally, after exhausting every effort to make this miserable job go away, you find that it has to be done and it has to be done by you—read on for your bonus strategy.

4. *Accept your fate.* Pitch in and give it your best attention. If it's a truly mechanical task that will take more wrist power than brainpower, put on some background music, treat yourself to coffee or cola (the margarita comes later), and slog away until it's done. If it's the sort of thing you can do in small chunks as you edit instead of all at once at the start, that might help prevent those emergency-room visits when the carpal tunnel gives out.

THE COMPLICATED TASK

If a mindless task can cause mental flake-out, a complicated task can cause mental overload. It requires your utmost care and concentration. Say an annual report you are editing has been prepared so that the source notes and credits to all the tables and figures are in footnotes that are numbered consecutively with those of the text.[1] No big deal—since the notes are linked electronically, you simply cut and paste into two separate hierarchies and all the notes will automatically renumber. The problem is that throughout the notes, instead of citing each source in full every time (Quentin Dinwiddie, *Zamboni Repair in the Home* [Omaha: Bizboom Press, 2007], appendix 42), the author refers the reader to previous citations by note number ("see n. 198"), and these references are hard-typed, not linked, and must be corrected to match the new numbers. Even that is fairly straightforward. But what if some of the full citations appear in table and figure notes, and others in the notes to the text?

I don't know about you, but when I face tasks like those, I have to fight a fear of getting so entangled in the corrections that I lose track of something and have to start all over again, rechecking. Let's call this Fear of the Major Undo.

Fear of the Undo can be familiar from other avenues of life. When I was a young mother, I joined a quilting circle. As perfectionists, quilters put copy editors in the shade. If something is the least bit out of whack, they will cheerfully rip out hours of stitching and start over. The process is the point, never mind if it takes years to finish. Quilters are so confident of a perfect product that they have a tradition of introducing a flaw into a quilt on purpose, in order not to offend the gods. When I joined this group, I had never been a patient seamstress. (If my mom were around to confirm that, she would probably just crack

1. Some of you will immediately understand and wince; perhaps the rest will take my word that this can cause major headaches. For instance, notes and credits formatted this way might not appear on the same pages as their respective tables and figures.

up laughing.) It was a great goal of mine to develop patience, both in quilting and in life. In time, I actually did achieve a Zenlike patience with a needle.

Unfortunately for me, that patience has never extended to any other aspect of life. Nothing puts me in more of a rage than having to revisit work I've already done in order to undo or redo it. Aside from the tedium and waste of time, I suffer knowing that it's nearly impossible to undo an editing decision with the same care and consistency with which I imposed it. I'm doomed to miss a few instances, and that means I will have introduced errors that might not have been there before. I will have done harm. A complicated task, in my view, is one in which the chances are high that you'll do harm. Mindless tasks, with time and patience, can usually be safely undone. The dangerous tasks I'm talking about now are not mindless, and because they involve concentrated decision-making to perform, they involve the same thought and concentration to undo.

This fear of having to undo or redo a complex chore—or even a mindless one—can be a great motivator to consider very carefully whether the task is truly necessary. I would urge you to ask yourself three questions about the current state of the manuscript before you begin surgery.

1. *Is it wrong?* Often the way a writer organizes/styles/formats his work isn't incorrect; it's just different. If the work follows a respected style guide and it would take a lot of time to rework in your preferred style, follow the four-step strategy I outlined for mindless tasks before you begin (automate, delegate, reevaluate, accept your fate). If it doesn't seem to follow any guide you're familiar with, but it's more or less consistent and makes sense, seriously consider leaving it alone.[2] The last several reference lists I've copyedited were each written in a

---

2. Not all editors have the option to ignore house style. The styling of source citations for most journals, for instance, is nonnegotiable. Fortunately, most journals also have fairly strict standards that writers must adhere to when submitting their work, so returning a substandard manuscript to the writer for another pass might be feasible.

unique hybrid of recognized styles. One author put all dates in parentheses; one put "ed." in parentheses; one reversed all author names in multiauthor works (Boyer, S. G.), while another reversed only the first author's name. All were nicely prepared, internally consistent, and unambiguous. I made whatever changes I could automate and left the rest.

2. Is it confusing? "Confusing" is a lesser form of "wrong" and calls for intervention. When all the legends to a series of pie charts list the percentages in alphabetical order instead of in order of quantity, it's not wrong—it just makes it harder for the reader to see at a glance who gets the biggest piece of the pie. When an author uses bibliography style for citations in the notes, inverting first name and last, putting periods and commas instead of semicolons between the elements, and so forth, a reader can barely tell where one citation begins and another ends:

32. Lynne, N. 1994. "The Chicken or the Egg?" In *Hysteron Proteron*. Ed. M. Parish. Cambridge, pp. 32–117, Dawn, R. 1958. "Spacing and Spacing Out: Unreasonable Reasonings." *Miseologus* 3:244–49.

This has to be fixed. But sometimes an unconventional method works just fine. If the pie charts are simple and the legends use color, they might work as they are. And in a one-of-a-kind bibliography, does it really matter where the date appears, or whether chapter titles are in quotation marks, if they're all done the same way and the facts are obvious? If you had all the time in the world to spend micro-tinkering such kinks into conformity with your rules, that would be great—but you don't. And while you're busy pouncing on every little dust bunny, you may be overlooking the monster under the bed, that is, more important problems with the content. Bottom line: if an odd style has logic and clarity, and if your institution gives you any measure of flexibility in the matter, leave well enough alone.

When I said as much in a recent reply to a query to the Q&A, the writer wrote back with some impatience:

Hmm, yes, and thank you for your reply. Is the following a fair summary of your message?

· Stop wasting time.

· Adhere to the style manual, except when you don't feel like it.

He pretty much nailed it—if we refine "when you don't feel like it" to "when it's not working for you."

3. Is it ugly? There is the occasional instance in which a writer's decision isn't wrong or confusing, but, aesthetically speaking, you know it will lie badly on the printed page and thereby hinder the reader. For instance, a surfeit of numbers in running text can be an eyesore and difficult to make sense of. The information might be better cast as a chart or table. On the other hand, material worked into tables is itself prone to ugliness: creating a table is far more difficult than criticizing or reshaping one that's already been made, and the creator of the table is often too close to the data to perceive the reader's problem with it. A long, skinny table might look better in two columns, for instance. Or sometimes a table's side and top headings ought to be flipped to allow more room for longer headings. People might naturally disagree about such matters if they ultimately depend more on personal taste than any kind of expertise, but the point remains that a copy editor should consider modifying features that will put the reader off, even if it calls for a bit of extra effort.

Once you've considered a complex editing issue and decided it must be done, lean on two of the virtues we talked about in part 1: carefulness and transparency. The first helps prevent mistakes; the second will help you check your work and undo it if you get into a fix. I narrowly escaped trouble when I meddled with the initial capping of quotations in a book about Shakespeare. I started out tracking my changes "like this" and "Like this" for the author's benefit. But after I had marked enough to give the author the idea of my method, I continued silently. If the author had wanted his original system reinstated (luckily, he opted for Chicago's style), I would have had to comb through the original manuscript, carefully searching for the Shakespeare quotations (scattered among many non-Shakespeare quotations), to find the errors. The transparency of redlining would have helped, but asking first (another kind of transparency) would have been better.

A third use of transparency is to send a sample of your editing that includes the reworked material in order to show the writer what you're doing before it's too late to change your mind.

WHEN WE GOOF

Sometimes—we must admit—we make mistakes, and there's no point in hoping that no one will notice. The only time I was able to make a mess of a manuscript without annoying the author was the time a severely dyslexic writer reviewed the editing and page proofs himself. Did I get away with murder? Not a chance. To my humiliation a reviewer wrote, "Finally, I must mention that this volume is poorly edited for a product from a major university press. Typographical errors and redundancies abound." At the time, I had many excuses and explanations for how, in spite of what I considered extraordinary efforts on my part to perfect that nightmare of a manuscript, more than the usual number of errors slipped into print. But there was no escaping the fact that it had been my responsibility. My biggest mistake was in not advising the publisher to hire a professional proofreader at the page-proof stage, knowing as I did that we wouldn't read it in-house and the author wasn't up to the task.

In that case, there was nothing I could do to put things right, but usually a major editing goof will be discovered when the writer or your supervisor reviews the editing, and you will have to fix it. Consider this part of the job and give it your best attention. Make apologies. Let the author see the cleaned-up version if there's time and your supervising editor agrees. In a book project, if the author is reviewing page proofs, that might be the best time for him to check that everything has been corrected.

Sometimes you will come to regret an editing decision in the middle of the job, before the writer ever has a chance to see it. If it's something that occurs frequently in the manuscript, something you can't easily fix by going back and searching, you're in trouble. Let's say that in a manuscript where "He" and "Him" are uppercased when referring to God, you decide to lowercase them. The writer doesn't seem to be expressing a theological point of view; the caps are out of place and misleading; lowercasing is your style; and—the clincher—the caps in the manuscript aren't consistently imposed. Then, later on, the pronouns proliferate. There are dozens and dozens of them, and every last one of them is capped. The author explains in a footnote that he caps them because his mother asked him to. On her deathbed.

Searching for lowercased pronouns like "he" and "him" is going to take awhile, but just be glad you have a chance to do it now.

Before you begin any time-consuming task like that, you should of course seriously ponder whether it really matters. Sometimes you might conclude that an issue doesn't deserve the time you would have to devote to sorting it out. Say you run into a sentence where the writer starts out using the pronoun "one" ("One might think that this is true . . ."), but switches to "you" partway (". . . in spite of everything you learned in kindergarten"). You change "one" to "you" and then notice another stray "one" further along in the paragraph. Pretty soon you're on a mission to rid the manuscript of "ones"—until you get distracted by something else. A few dozen pages later, you remember and start worrying that you let a few get by you. Aargh. Is this important? (No.) Is it worth your time to revisit the issue? (No.) Will the author notice? (Probably, since your previous hen tracks will give you away.)

A good strategy in such a case is to mention the matter when you hand over the work for review. That way, if the author cares enough, he can keep an eye out for it as he reads. To help prevent his dismay, point out why the styling is optional or the issue not that important. ("Early in the manuscript, I paid attention to your use of 'you' vs. 'one,' but at some point I seem to have lost interest in the matter, probably because there's no compelling reason to avoid the variation, other than within a given sentence. If you care to put back anything I changed in this regard or make further changes for the sake of consistency, please feel free.") Don't make a big deal out of small matters—if it were a big deal, you would have gone back and fixed it. ("I think it's sometimes good to repeat the poem number when you resume discussion of a poem after a digression. I wasn't rigid about it, lest the text become riddled with unneeded references; I added them whenever I found myself thinking 'wait—which poem were we in?' Add more if you like, or strike mine if you think they're intrusive.")

Sometimes, no matter how hard you try, you aren't going to be able to rationalize away an editing error that ends up in the hands of the author. Not long ago I edited a novel—a rarity for me—in which the main character professed to be a famous (historically real) Spanish explorer from the past. Although the character's name was properly accented on the title page, the accent was inconsistently applied throughout the manuscript. I wasn't surprised—many writers omit accents when they type, either overlooking them or slothfully assuming they'll be put in by someone later. So right away I zapped them all into place, hundreds of them, with a lightning search-and-replace. I didn't give it another thought until I received the editing back from the author with a kindly explanation of why it was important to remove the accents I had added. Remember—this was fiction. It turned out that the author hadn't overlooked a thing and had not a slothful bone in his body, but in his meticulous and ingenious way, had thought very carefully about why the name should be accented in certain contexts and not others. We debated whether this distinction would be lost on readers, but like much good fiction, this novel was built upon many such subtleties, the sum of which provided a delightful complexity. I had goofed; the issue was important; I had no choice but to take the time to remove the accents, one by one.

· · ·

So far in this chapter, if I have skirted the further dangers that can arise when we try to automate complex tasks, it's not because I take it for granted that each of you has mastered your word processor.

Rather, it's because I think word-processing issues deserve a chapter all their own. Read on.

A / Well, if you don't allow the serial comma at all, you will at times be stuck with situations like the following hypothetical dedication page that our managing editor likes to cite: "With gratitude to my parents, Mother Teresa and the pope." (Maybe that example will help you change your company's policy.)

CHAPTER SEVEN

Know Thy Word Processor

Q / Is there an accepted practice for the use of emoticons that include an opening or closing parenthesis as the final token within a set of parentheses? Should I (1) incorporate the emoticon into the closing of the parentheses (such as in this case. :-) (2) simply leave the emoticon up against the closing parenthesis, ignoring the bizarre visual effect (producing a doubled-chin effect :-)) (3) put a space or two (like this: :-)) (4) or avoid the situation by using a similar emoticon (:-D), placing the emoticon elsewhere, or doing without it?

If, in copyediting, a little knowledge is a dangerous thing, the same is doubly so in word processing, where lightning can strike with one peck of your pinky. While you are making it your business to master your chosen style rules, you must make a similar priority of mastering your word-processing application. With the debut of every new version, word-processing software becomes more powerful—capable of automating many vexing tasks—but also capable of making the most exquisite mess of your work.

As the mother of twenty-somethings, I was recently surprised to realize that typical college students—even computer-savvy techie types—are not necessarily competent at word processing. They know how to type a paper, possibly insert some footnotes or endnotes, and add page numbers. They know how to jazz up a document with funky fonts and colors. They might have played around enough to discover the prefab heading styles and margin settings.

As a copy editor, you must know far, far more to do your job efficiently. Entire books are available detailing the how-tos of word processing, so that is not my purpose here. Because readers of this book will work in a variety of applications, and because software capabilities change so rapidly, I will focus more generally on the pitfalls of editing on-screen and how we can cope with them.

ME? READ A MANUAL?

There are countless ways to learn a new application or refine your skills in one you're already using, but my first recommendation is that you read a commercially published manual rather than the documentation that came with your software. Four out of five techies agree that you need a manual at least 1.5 inches thick.[1] To decide which guide you want, browse through several; look up something you already know how to do, and see whether the instructions are clear and mesh with your knowledge. Once you've chosen, read everything that pertains to your work and do the exercises. Keep the book at hand as a reference so you can look up the solutions to problems you encounter while you work. I guarantee you won't regret it—the savings in time and grief will more than repay the investment.[2] Alternatively, you might take a class or find a tutor.

Learning to use keyboard shortcuts instead of motoring around the screen with a mouse is a good place to start improving your skills, because shortcuts are fun and easy and can save you time and physical pain from mouse-steering. Many shortcuts are already built into your

1. This is exactly the kind of statement that must be supported by a credible source citation. [Note to copy editor: I *promise* I'll get you this by next week!]

2. Hilary Powers has written a gem of a guide, *Making Word Work for You: An Editor's Intro to a Tool of the Trade* (New York: Editorial Freelancers Association, 2007). You can download it inexpensively at http://www.lulu.com/content/1175135. A more comprehensive manual is the *Microsoft Word 2007 Bible*, by Herb Tyson (Indianapolis: Wiley, 2007). It measures 2.0 inches thick and includes a searchable CD-ROM.

word-processing application, and you can assign your own as well. With shortcuts you can navigate quickly within and between documents, choose items from menus, apply and remove formatting, cut and paste text, expand and collapse windows—really almost anything you like—all by tapping a couple of keys and involving no contact with rodents.

When you venture past the basics of word processing, the amount of information will be overwhelming, so take notes on the operations that you most want to learn. Start by keeping instructions on your desk for two or three new tricks at a time. Post them on a sticky near your monitor. When those become second nature, move on.

Assuming it will take you some time to work through your manual, use other resources in the meantime to troubleshoot word-processing challenges as they arise. The help files that are included in your software application contain vast archives of instruction (if you can figure out how to negotiate the menu). Your search engine is also a powerful tool. Typing keywords of a problem into Google or Yahoo often will turn up a solution. I'll give you an example. Say your author has typed her three-page table of contents in all caps, so that a typical title looks like this:

SIMULTANEOUS DEVELOPMENT WITH MECHANICAL DESIGN

This will never do. It's a rare design that will stand for the shouting of all caps anywhere at all, let alone three pages of them. In the Pencil Age, we would have marked this by hand, putting three little lines under each letter that should appear capped, since typesetters are not expected to know the rules for upper- and lowercasing in titles. Even today I suspect many editors would submit hand-marked hard copy rather than make all the tedious changes electronically. But Googling "MS Word shortcuts" takes you to numerous websites where you can read that hitting Shift + F3 is a shortcut for changing case. Highlighting all three pages and hitting Shift + F3 will lowercase everything in an instant:

simultaneous development with mechanical design

Hitting the same keys again will change the case to headline caps:

Simultaneous Development With Mechanical Design

To make further adjustments, put your cursor in the words that need lowercasing (like *With*) and tap Shift + F3. Or better, use the search-and-replace feature to lowercase *The*, *And*, and other common words. (Do this one at a time, lest you lowercase words that begin a title.) You've just saved yourself retyping three pages of text. And there are dozens—hundreds?—of shortcuts like this.

There are excellent sites online that give word-processing tips and tricks. The Editorium offers downloadable macros that make quick work of tasks like cleaning up tabs and spacing, unembedding notes, and turning automatic bullets or numbering into real ones.[3] Experiment with recording your own macros for chores you repeat often.

Finally, don't forget human resources: the advantage of asking a fellow copy editor when you're stuck is that, unlike your computer, he knows your job and will understand exactly what you are trying to do—and what you don't want to happen. You may also subscribe to a listserv of editors who will respond to a posted query. When you post a question, consider waiting for more than one response. Sometimes an added caveat will save you from bad advice.

COLLISION INSURANCE: FIVE WAYS TO AVOID THE BIG CRASH

Learning techniques to speed up your work through computer shortcuts can be intoxicating, but remember, you're the designated driver here. Who among us has never in haste saved the wrong ver-

---

3. http://www.editorium.com/. There are many free resources here: Editorium's "Advanced Find and Replace for Microsoft Word" looks complicated on first reading, but if you have already figured out how to do wildcard searches in Word, going to this next level is not really so difficult, and learning it could add years to your life.

sion over the right one, or recognized too late an ill-conceived global search-and-replace? I have personal knowledge of a work that contained references to the Paris Peach Conference, and another whose author caught in the nick of time several mentions of trouble with the Genitals in his work on Jewish-Gentile relations. And then there was the astrophysics text where two fluid elements in "causal contact" came to be in "casual contact" (which, I now know, is not at all the same thing). If you've been lucky this far, maybe it's because you know five important practices of e-file management.

1. *Labels and folders.* Although it's possible to get through life with all your documents in one vast folder in your file manager, why would anyone do that, when it's so easy to create discrete folders, and folders within folders, and folders within folders within folders? (I could go on, but then you'd think I'm neurotic about filing within folders.) When you get original copy, create a working folder with the project name, say, Snowden MS, and within that, a folder called Snowden Original. If it makes you feel safer, lock the original files so they can't be altered, but in any case, make copies to put in the working folder; these are the files you'll use for editing.[4] At this point, if the original consists of more than one document, I combine them into a single working file. I also create a single superfile called Original Combined, in case I need to search the original later. (Combining files is quick and easy to do using keyboard shortcuts.) Depending on your software, it can be faster to search within a single file than across several. Besides, I prefer the search function within Microsoft Word to that of a file manager like Windows Explorer; it never startles me with bearded wizards or scratching dogs.

Likewise, you can create folders within a project folder: Text,

4. There is a powerful feature within Microsoft Word that allows you to save "versions" of your documents, which you may or may not find useful. These versions are part of the document itself, not separate copies. They allow you to consult or revert to previous stages of the editing. You can save a version manually at any time, or you can ask Word to record a version automatically whenever you close your document. You can label the versions, retrieve them, compare them. It's another type of backup, with the critical differences that the resulting file is gigantic, and if it is lost, all the versions are lost along with it.

Tables, Figures, Correspondence. The Snowden folder can be put in a folder called Manuscripts, along with other projects that you're working on. Besides the Manuscripts folder, create folders that pertain to your work: Administration, Clippings, Freelancers, Invoices, Meetings, Purchase Orders, Reference, Reviews, Tech. I admit that I was once somewhat enslaved to my filing system, and at some point, it probably does become counterproductive to nest the folders too deeply, so create your filing hierarchy in a way that allows you to locate what you need quickly, and if you find it's getting out of hand, well, maybe there's a twelve-step program for you.

2. *Trial runs*. When you're about to try something extra tricky while editing a manuscript, don't gamble with your working document. Save it under a new name, like Test 1, and see how it works out before you inflict it for keeps. I always create a test file before I carry out actions that consist of a series of steps difficult to undo, knowing that if I fail to notice certain kinds of slips, my document is toast. I usually save the test file in "read-only" format so I can use it the next time I need one.

One danger I've run into with test files: I get up to find coffee, stop to chat with Joe in Production, answer my ringing phone before I get back to the monitor—and forget that the file open on the screen is a test file. Before I learned to use the read-only format, I once worked for an hour before I realized I'd been editing the wrong version of my manuscript. Another time, I didn't label the test file clearly as such, and accidentally saved it over the correct version when I was in a hurry to finish. I wanted to kill somebody. To prevent confusion now, I like to color the font in my test file. (You can do this with the original file for the same reason.) I find olive green to be soothing.

3. *Version control*. The trauma of accidentally replacing a current file with an older one can happen any time you need to consult an older version for some reason. Your clearly labeled documents and folders help you avoid this sort of mistake. Using the read-only format for files you want to preserve is even better insurance, assuming you save early and often as you work, because as soon as you try to save, you'll be alerted that the file cannot be altered. For each project, I keep sepa-

rate folders for the original, the redlined (or edited) files, and the final files. Occasionally there are interim stages that have their own labels and folders, such as files that I have cleaned up before sending to a freelancer, or the files that she returns to me.

At Chicago, most edited manuscripts still go to the authors in the form of hard-copy printouts, but that is changing so quickly that by the time you are reading this, it may no longer be the case. If you are sending electronic files to a writer for vetting, it's essential to keep straight who has the working copy. If the author is busy making changes and corrections at the same time you're adding final tweaks, even if both of you are scrupulous about tracking every change, you will have confusion. When I send e-files to an author with the idea that she will use the tracking feature to make her corrections, I remind her that I have the working copy, and that if she changes anything without tracking it, I won't see it, and it won't make it into the final book. It's not necessarily the whole truth, because after I'm able to examine the vetted files from the author, I might very well decide to use them as the working copy. But it's important to me to retain the option. Depending on the nature of the author's tasks, you might decide to lock in the tracking feature so the author cannot turn it off.

4. *Transparency.* An added point of going to so much trouble with folders and labels and versions is that occasionally someone other than you might have to find something in your computer. Although that might happen rarely, it's a certainty that someone else will handle your e-files when they're in final form and it's time to send them into production. For that reason, you should label everything clearly and get rid of any hidden electronic litter that could interfere with clean typesetting.

5. *Backup.* My son Ben has worked on and off in computer tech support and has heard quite a few war stories from the veterans. He told me that one of the first things he learned was how to handle the arrogance and rage of crash victims, often directed at the technician. He was advised to reassure the person, and if he could get the computer up and running, say, "Okay, great—no problem. If you'll just give me your backup disks, we'll put everything back the way it was." Then in-

evitably came the victim's deer-in-the-headlights face as she realized whose fault it was that there were no backup disks.

I know there's no need to belabor the point. Back up your work as often as you need in order not to slit your wrists when you lose it. For me, this means every day as I log off. U of C Press has an off-site server I copy files to, and for good measure I also keep a USB drive attached to my CPU. Because it literally takes only a few seconds, I copy my work for the day to both drives (backup software will do this for you automatically, if you prefer), and occasionally I take the USB drive home to transfer files to my computer there. Sometimes I e-mail files as attachments from my work computer to my home. If you work only at home, you might consider renting space online to store backup copies of your work. A related good habit is to press "Save" often as you work. For me, it's become a sort of unconscious twitch.

RESISTING COMPULSION

There are many obvious reasons to edit text on a computer instead of on paper. It allows us to add and delete copy cleanly, to make our editing visible or invisible as we choose, to take care of repetitive tasks efficiently and consistently. We can e-mail documents to others both in-house and out, and the finished document can go to typesetting with the expectation of fewer typos in page proofs than otherwise. Although in the early days of electronic word processing most of us probably believed it would save time and paper (and therefore money), I doubt that many of us find that to be true. We print because we can— I see no evidence of a green movement in my office. If the printout is missing page numbers, are you going to number them in with a pencil, or simply print them over again? We print the original manuscript, the edited version, and the final version, not to mention photocopies for this or that. And as for saving time? My editing schedules have not changed significantly in twenty years. The time we save in automating tasks, we lose in having to prepare the e-files for typesetting.[5] What we save in hand marking, we lose in a hundred other little tasks that we do because it's so easy we can't resist.

And that is the challenge: to rein in our compulsive tendencies in favor of efficiency. Just because we can, doesn't mean we should. It bears repeating: if you are about to embark on a time-consuming task, remember your three-step emergency mantra: automate, delegate, re-evaluate. It's possible to accumulate hours of wasted time out of compulsion and ignorance. One editor I know didn't like the way Word uses superscripted note numbers in the notes pane instead of placing them full-sized on the line with a period, so one by one, for each of hundreds of notes, she highlighted the number, formatted it to Not Superscript (using her mouse and the menu), and typed a period after it—a chore that she could have accomplished for the entire document in less than twenty seconds using keyboard commands.[6]

We'll return to the topic of our compulsions later. For now, let's continue thinking about efficiency and the reasons we need to stop wasting time. In the next chapter, let's think about deadlines.

A / Until academic standards decline enough to accommodate the use of emoticons, I'm afraid *CMOS* is unlikely to treat their styling, since the manual is aimed primarily at scholarly publications. And the problems you've posed in this note give us added incentive to keep our distance. (But I kind of like that double-chin effect.)

5. A common complaint among copy editors is that our responsibilities have been extended to include a great deal of preproduction work that we are not trained for and have little interest in. The formula in my department is to add an extra 20 percent to the estimate of editing hours for cleaning up the original files (stripping out formatting, odd spacing, stray tabs, etc.), assigning typesetting codes, and updating the e-files after the writer has reviewed the editing.

6. Okay—I will admit that this was me. But it was a long time ago, and I recognized that I had a problem and sought help.

CHAPTER EIGHT

The Living Deadline

Q / Please answer as soon as possible as I am on a deadline.

Q / My deadline is June 30—so I need to get moving.

Q / Please answer asap we are on a deadline.

Q / I'm on a deadline and need some help.

Q / I'm under a tight deadline here.

Q / And yes, I'm under deadline.

Q / My deadline looms.

The writer Douglas Adams famously claimed to love deadlines: "I love deadlines," he said. "I like the whooshing sound they make as they fly by."

Isn't that adorable.

We love writers, and we indulge them for their quirky, creative genius. But the rest of us have to meet our deadlines, and the letters to the Q&A attest to that in force. Some schedules are more firm than others—obviously, the timing of publications like newspapers and magazines allows little wiggle room. Although most book deadlines have at least some room to slide—and many do, by days, weeks, or in the worst cases even years—that is never the goal, and a copy editor who consistently misses deadlines will mark herself as incompetent and unreliable.

Delays in publishing are often outside the copy editor's control, even when the manuscript is in her own hands. The electronic files may be corrupted. Parts of the manuscript might be missing. A writer sends late-breaking information that must be added. Even after the editing is finished, when the editor is preparing the manuscript for production, the design specifications might be late, or permissions to use material incomplete, or an illustration found to be substandard. The author may be unreachable. (One editor told me about a delay over some missing references that the author couldn't send because his wife was holding his research hostage in the end stages of their divorce.) Sometimes a minor delay compounds as it precipitates another: say a photographer who agreed to a photo shoot by a certain date is stalled by your publicity department's failure to find the right props; the photographer is booked with other projects, thereby turning a week's delay into a month's delay.

Hang-ups outside your control are just that; all you can do is make your team or your supervisor aware of them. Given the short schedules at newspapers and magazines, delays can deep-six a project altogether. If you aren't directly responsible for the holdup of a given piece, your prompts and gentle naggings might be the only thing saving it from being scrapped. It can be especially tempting for editors of book manuscripts to shrug at deadlines when it begins to seem as though a project has little chance of delivery at the targeted date no matter how watchful you are. But that attitude is damaging both to the publishing team and to yourself. The economic damage is predictable: seasonal lists and budgets are planned to accommodate average delays. If everyone slacks off because "delays don't matter," the average delay will grow, and that's not good for the financial health of your company.

In more personal terms, inattention to deadlines will inconvenience everyone who follows you in the assembly line. You will become—unpopular.

To manage your deadlines, become proficient in three skills: prioritizing, organizing, and documentizing.[1]

---

1. If you aren't reading this, it's because it didn't make it past the copy editor. [Note to copy editor: *Oxford English Dictionary*, 2nd ed.: "documentize, *v. trans.* **a.** To teach,

PRIORITIZING: FOUR QUESTIONS TO HELP YOU PLAN

Copy editors have a million things to do. Either we handle several over-lapping projects, or we handle multiple tasks within a single project. If we aren't freelancers ourselves, we supervise freelancers. My to-do list on a typical day might include sending page proofs to an author, reading an index manuscript, putting a finished manuscript into production, cleaning up a manuscript that's come back from an author, making notes on a new project for an editorial meeting, checking permission letters against an author's figure credits—never mind actually reading the manuscript I'm in the middle of editing. Your list will be similarly full.

You can't do all those things in one day, even if they're due. But you do have some choices: you can freak out and take a sick day; you can stay up all night drinking coffee; or you can figure out which chores are most urgent, get them done, and then call up a beau and go dancing. You pick.

Triaging your projects can be agonizing unless you develop some guidelines. Here are four questions to weigh when you can't decide what to do first.

1. *Is it next?* A good rule of thumb is that, all else being equal, the project that's nearest publication gets the attention. That is, if the agenda for tomorrow's board of directors' meeting lands on your desk just when you were getting ready to tackle next quarter's news-letter to investors, the agenda wins. If the Kimball index lands in your tray when you were getting ready to look at the Hannigan man-uscript just back from the author, the index trumps the manuscript for your attention. When typesetting is involved, it's more likely that end-stage delays will inconvenience others. By that time, folks in the production and publicity departments will have assumed much of the responsibility for getting the title delivered and promoted on time, and they're probably juggling twice as many projects as you. If you hold things up, you're likely to interfere with their typesetting

---

instruct, give a lesson to. **b.** To furnish with evidence." Yes, it's obsolete, but I needed a word with *zing*.]

and promotion schedules. At the start of a project, however, it's all yours.

2. Is it most important? For whatever reason, some projects are more important than others, either because they're big money spinners or because the client or author is a heavyweight. When you bump one task for another for the reason of importance, remember that it's not necessary to explain in detail to a writer or client the reasons his work isn't progressing as planned. After all, what can you say? "I'm so sorry about the delay—I was attending to a more important project"? Unless it's your boss who's asking, just apologize for the delay; don't explain: "I'm sorry this is taking longer than expected; if all goes well, I should be able to send you everything by the end of the week. I'll keep you posted."

3. Is it most urgent? Magazine and journal articles with rigid delivery dates can't wait. Corporations have legal imperatives to publish certain reports at set times of the fiscal year. Books can also have important delivery dates, planned for optimal marketing around a holiday, annual conference, or textbook season. Or a piece might be rushed because it treats a political or popular issue that's hot this minute but doomed to fade. (Remember that book on the Reykjavík Salmon Summit of 1988? Me neither.)

Short, urgent tasks (anything with a "Rush" tag on it, for example) should get your immediate attention. A task can also be urgent if holding it up will cause a consequent delay; for instance, if you don't get the edited copy to a writer by Friday, he'll be unable to look at it for two weeks. Recently I had two urgent tasks and decided which one would have to wait, not realizing that the designer who would handle it after me was leaving on vacation the next day. Too late, I wished I'd e-mailed her to say, "I'm not sure I can get to the Timberlake revises today—is tomorrow just as good?"

4. Is it the right thing to do? Sometimes a task might not be the most urgent or important, but you promised it in such a way that your conscience won't let you shove it aside. Those are tough choices, but you'll sleep better if you honor your promise. You know what I mean: one of those desperately caring authors who sweats blood over every decision e-mails you to ask whether it might be better to convert tables 2, 6, 32, and 34 into text, and you promise to look at them as soon as possible, and you know he's wringing his hands until it's decided. If you're displacing an important or urgent task, you might have to put in some overtime until you're caught up.

Some caveats: First, don't make a habit of promising anything, especially in response to demanding personalities: just tell Maynard in Production that you'll get to his pet task as soon as you can, and be specific about when, if possible. And second, when you communicate an expected delay, it's better to tell than ask. If you ask ("Do you mind if that's a few days late?"), you might not get the answer you're hoping for. Unless you're fishing for information that will help you order your tasks, it's better to simply say or write, "The Herrmann piece is going to be a few days late. I'm aiming to get it to you on Tuesday next week." If it turns out that your delay will cause a major problem, you'll no doubt hear about it, and you can always reconsider.

Finally, be aware of the way you work best, and take that into account when faced with competing tasks from various projects. If you get confused flipping back and forth between the works of different writers (because it involves switching your brain between two very different styles—or worse, only slightly different styles), try not to do that. Instead, give the Oaks project your full attention until you've done all you can with it. Remind yourself that keeping a clear head within each document is essential if you want to serve the reader well.

ORGANIZING

This section is a tough one, but I'd really like you to read it. Think of this as the vegetable section. If you work in publishing, being organized is good for your health. If you're already a well-organized editor, take a vitamin and skip this part. If you're a veggie lover, all the better.

An old Chinese proverb that happens to feature a vegetable (well, technically a fruit, but I don't want this to be the fruit section) says, "One cannot manage too many affairs: like pumpkins in the water, one pops up while you try to hold down the other." The trouble is, we've got the pumpkins. The question is, how to keep track of them.

Organization is a personal matter. Some like nothing better than to poke at pumpkins, and others would rather just hang on to one at a time. As you know by now, I tend to be a hyperfiling, to-do-list type of gal, but I have known other systems to work. Everyone knows someone who organizes by the "stack" method. During the years I worked acquiring children's books, one colleague was famous for this. No one could imagine how she found anything in the piles of paper on her desk, on the credenza, on the filing cabinet, and on the floor. Yet I never knew her to lose anything, and she was more prompt than anyone in returning manuscripts I wanted her opinion on. She said she returned things quickly so she wouldn't lose them—her own style of efficiency.

That said, there are a few organizing tools that are indispensable to any professional. *Lists* give you a picture of the short term, *schedules* show the longer-term view, and *logs* keep track of what you've already done. All three are worth a closer look. Let's make a list.

1. *Lists.* A simple to-do list is an excellent aid. Think of it as the editor's broccoli. I keep mine in a Word document that has a shortcut icon on my computer desktop, and I click it open first thing after I look at my e-mail every morning and I keep it open all day. Whenever I need to remind myself to do something, I type it in, more or less in order of urgency. I can delete tasks when they're done or rearrange their order.

Young readers, stop rolling your eyes! ("Like, who could forget this stuff?") Those pushing middle age or older will be nodding in recognition of my wisdom. Although I tend to list large tasks (Go over Lewis permissions; read Woodward front matter), a list can be as detailed as you like and in whatever form suits you. Some of my colleagues prefer to write tasks on a calendar, and others paste yellow stickies around their monitors and bookshelves. More than one has mentioned leaving voice-mail reminders for herself. Whatever works.

The advantage of my little written list is that one glance at the top of it tells me what to do next.

2. *Schedules*. Here at the U of C Press, we have an amazing online schedule that allows each of us to see our project deadlines in any number of displays tailored to the information we request. My favorite is a list of the tasks I'm responsible for in the next two weeks, in alphabetical order by author. I open it each morning to get a look at what's on the horizon. In contrast to my to-do list, which prioritizes tasks currently on my desk and helps me plan my day, the schedule includes upcoming tasks that are out of my hands at the moment, prompting me to check in with authors and colleagues concerning their progress. If the schedule shows that an edited manuscript is due back from the author in a week, I might shoot a quick e-mail in that direction. ("Just checking in. Have you had a chance to look at the editing? Do you expect to have it back to me next week?") If a manuscript is slated for typesetting soon and I don't have everything I need, that's a prompt to send reminders. ("Dorman is ready to go as soon as I have design specs. Just wanted to let you know.")

If you don't have a high-tech schedule to consult, creating even a rudimentary one will help you meet your deadlines. A list on paper, a calendar, or an e-file like my to-do list—all are handy guides to what's happening when.

3. *Logs*. I'm going to mention logs here because they are good organizing tools, even though they tend to focus on what's finished, rather than what's not, and in that way they aren't especially relevant to deadline control. Administrators keep logs out of necessity—part of their job is to account for how much work was done and how long it took and how much it cost. Freelancers need logs, probably best kept in the form of spreadsheets, to keep track of clients, fees, and income from each job. Software can sort the information in various displays: jobs done for a particular client, total income from that client, or whatever is needed—all very handy at tax time. Project managers, likewise, can keep a spreadsheet log of freelancers, with dates in and out, rates per hour or page, invoice totals, contact information, and anything else that is useful.

My log is a personal tool and very simple. At the end of each day, I type what I did. Here's one day (if my log doesn't make sense to you, yours will): "Feb. 20. Gilfoyle ed. notes. C&P final lasers. Edit Brown, to 216. Mtg. w/ JT, SMH, & PDK re Baker schedule."

I was inspired to start my log a couple of years ago when I seemed to be in a malaise: at the end of one day, I was ashamed at how little I'd done—well, we all have those days. But I knew it hadn't been just that day, and I resolved to start accounting to myself for my time. What began as self-help, however, evolved into more than a motivational tool as I found myself referring to it for information that had expired from my schedules and to-do lists. I often consult the log when I need to recall a project that has been on the back burner for a while before contacting an author or nudging a coworker. (I keep my log right below my to-do list, so it's all in one e-file.)

Altogether, lists, schedules, and logs take only a minute or two each day to update and are among the best possible uses of your time, considering the amount of time and confusion they can save. Plus, I promise they will give you whiter teeth and stronger bones.

DOCUMENTING

Even when all your pumpkins are under control, they're only yours temporarily, and at some point you'll be handing them off. Keeping others apprised of fluctuations in your schedules is an important part of managing deadlines. It's no help for you to finish early if the stage isn't set for the next act. And if you're running late, the person waiting on you wants to know it sooner rather than later. If you're part of a publishing team, then, you need to know what's promised to whom, and when. And because such things can change unpredictably, you need to keep track of everyone's latest requests, promises, and updates so you can refer to them regularly.

E-mail has become the most common and efficient way to keep records of this sort. Letters and phone calls are sometimes necessary—even preferable, for the personal touch—and certainly you can file the former and keep notes on the latter, but e-mail takes up less space and can be speedily searched. For this reason, I see e-mail management as the best tool for documenting deadline-related information.

Whole books have been published on the subject of managing e-mail, but for the copy editor, the basics can be boiled down to three: (1) order, (2) discipline, and (3) etiquette. The first two are relevant here; I'll talk about etiquette in the next chapter.

E-mail order. You would think that the virtues of sorting e-mail messages into folders in the same way you file other electronic documents would be obvious, but I'm regularly surprised to learn that an otherwise methodical person chooses to keep all her messages in one, extravagant, yards-long list in her in-box. How many times have I stood waiting for information while someone scrolled and clicked and scrolled and clicked, muttering, "I know it's here somewhere"? Creating separate folders along the same lines as the ones described in the chapter on word processing allows you to click through recent correspondence efficiently. Even though you can search your in-box as easily as you can search a stack of folders, perhaps even more easily, a search for almost any given term will return results from various projects. Losing information is only one problem. Another is that unless you are scrupulous about reading and responding to every message before it gets bumped off the bottom of the in-box screen, soon there will be a number of messages that are out of sight—and out of mind. Invisible and unanswered. Which leads to the next point.

E-mail discipline. Whether you read your incoming messages the minute they arrive or once an hour or once a day, staying on top of them is imperative if you want to maintain good work relationships and keep abreast of news that affects your deadlines. I find it appalling when my second query about something is met with "I'm sorry—I must have missed your first message somehow." It's one of those rare areas of work etiquette that I believe to be nonnegotiable: when someone sends you a work-related message, you read it and respond. The temptation is strong to delay answering until you can write at length, until you can look something up, until you can report that the task is finished—but of course by then the message has fallen off your screen and out of your brain. And don't tell me you don't have time. In five seconds or less, you can hit Reply, type "Thanks" or "Done" or "I'm on it" or "Will do," and hit Send. "More to come!" and "Stay tuned . . ." take another couple of seconds at most. If you aren't on such easy terms with a particular correspondent, it takes only a few more seconds to add a bit of formality: "Nan, I'm sorry I'm in a rush at the moment, but I'll make this a priority—I'll get back to you asap. Best, Carol."

A system that works well for me is to use my in-box only for messages I haven't finished with. In effect, it's another to-do list. Everything else gets trashed or filed immediately. I also sort through the out-box frequently, and I never allow it to grow beyond one pane's worth. (I'm sorry if I'm beginning to sound superior, but I can't help it. I am the queen of e-mail discipline.)

A / Because of the large number of questions we receive, we are not able to answer each question individually. Please check the Q&A monthly to see whether your question has been selected to be featured—and answered—on the site. If you're on deadline, phone 911.

CHAPTER NINE

That Damned Village

Q / A colleague of mine insists on using a comma before "while."

Q / Our new publications director insists on leaving in or adding unnecessary *thats*.

Q / A copy editor in my office insists on adding "of" after the word "all."

Q / I have a colleague who insists on using "as well as" at the beginning of a sentence.

Q / One of my colleagues insists on using the format 5th February, 2005.

"My boss/colleague/coworker/secretary insists on . . ." How many times have I read that opening line? Reading the mail, I wonder if there is a single office in America (other than mine) where colleagues get along. It seems to be an unfortunate fact that when people share writing tasks, there will be disagreement. And with disagreement, evidently, there is tension.

Almost any piece of prose that is subjected to copyediting is also subjected to scrutiny by others involved in the process of publishing it. Copy is passed from editor to writer and back again, then through project editors or managing editors on the way to typesetting. Designers may question content that affects the design; typesetters might question seeming inconsistencies. Jacket copy or ad copy is routed past a dozen red pencils, and everyone has an opinion. Copy editors, often at the bottom of the status heap, must negotiate with colleagues in order to protect the work of the writer on its way to the reader.

Even if you're freelancing at home, you will work with, and inevitably disagree with, an assigning editor. Glean what you can from this chapter, and be patient—the next chapter is especially for you.

In a workplace there is often a prevailing culture. If you're lucky, your coworkers are genial and collaborative and quick to give credit where it's due. When I was young, I worked at a magazine where the elderly assistant managing editor was always falling asleep at his desk. One of my coworkers was so concerned about embarrassing him during a nap, she would phone him and hang up before going to his office. (Historical note: This was in the days of jarring ring tones and no caller ID.)

I'm going to assume that this level of courtesy doesn't exist everywhere. Your coworkers may be competitive and ready to point fingers when there's trouble. Whatever your work environment, there are some commonsense guidelines to live by at work that I can pretty well guarantee you won't regret.

NO EDITOR IS AN ISLAND

If only you could do everything yourself.

Ha! Not only do we depend on our colleagues at work; we can't possibly do all the things they do, and often enough we don't have any real understanding of how they do it. It's easy to assume that delays caused by others are the result of incompetence or laziness. If you're the anxious type, such hang-ups can be stressful and irritating, and if you're not watchful, they can lead to accusations and arguments.

When it comes to laying blame for delays, that miraculous online schedule I described above does the finger-pointing in my office: since it publicly keeps track of and displays every stage of a book's progress, everyone can see where a project is languishing. It doesn't, however, always display the *reasons*. That can be a good thing, if the reason you haven't finished editing Crankhauer is that you met someone cute at eHarmony, or annoying if the reason you're late sending out Purdy's page proofs is that the typesetters missed a chapter.

The point is, you can't always know the reasons a colleague is holding things up, either. When glitches seem to be the fault of someone other than yourself, there's no need to get defensive or name names. Just send reminders and queries in order to notify others who are waiting further along. We've already covered the mechanics of using lists, schedules, and logs to keep track of who's on first. What's left is to focus on effective communication with others. I said my advice would be commonsense, so here it is: Play nicely, and work through channels.

Let's expand a bit.

PLAYING NICELY

There are approaches to office behavior that will stand you in good stead with your coworkers and grease the wheels of every negotiation, whether in spoken interactions or in written communications, specifically e-mailing.

Straight shooting in personal confrontations. When things are going well, it's easy to be cordial and cooperative in our dealings with colleagues. It's when there's trouble that we reveal our worst selves. (That same sweet colleague from the magazine who tiptoed around the narcoleptic assistant manager used to wake up the rest of us squabbling with the editor whose copy she had to fact-check. She remembers a time he confronted her at her desk while she was on the phone with a writer. While they yelled insults at each other, she could hear the writer through the phone whimpering, "No! No! Stop—please! Don't fight! Please stop!")

So who hasn't flung an angry word or resorted to sarcasm in a tense office situation, or deflected blame to someone else behind his back, or resorted to manipulative tactics in order to get what we want? And does it ever help? It's more likely that a calm and fair statement of a problem, without exaggeration or finger-pointing, will enlist another's cooperation. ("Linda, I'm worried about having the Henry project by October 1 in time for that conference. Is there any way you can get this off your desk in the next day or two?")

I remember an incident at my first job when I flounced into the managing editor's office, slapped a piece of marked-up copy onto his desk, and said, "I'm sorry, but I can't work this way! Either Mrs. R. goes, or I go!" I was lucky he didn't call my bluff and hand me a pink slip right then and there. Instead, he burst out laughing, which made me laugh, too. But it's probably a rare tantrum that ends as well as that one did. On the contrary, such behavior not only makes us look bad; it tends to escalate a disagreement. In the same situation today, I would go to Mrs. R. herself and say, "I'd like to work with you in a better way. Can we talk?"

Negative attitudes, like anger, add to office stress. So monitor yours. In a competitive environment, you can refuse to compete. If Tom receives praise or bonuses for productivity, reexamine your work habits and look for your own inefficiencies, with the goal to improve yourself, not to outdo Tom. In fact, you might ask him what his secret is. In a back-stabbing environment where others withhold information or show each other up in meetings, don't play that game. Be generous and open with your knowledge. Make sure you're up-to-date on everything before you represent a team, and give a private heads-up to a colleague who might be embarrassed by not knowing something you know. ("Barb, I'm making up the Jensen notes for the meeting, and my file says not all the art is in. If you have it now, I won't mention it at the meeting.") Observe courtesies that cost you nothing. Watch yourself for little habits like frowning when someone drops work on your desk. You might just as well smile and thank him for the delivery, even if you both know you don't really mean it. Without being a Pollyanna about it, you can do your part to foster courtesy and collegiality in your workplace.

E-mail etiquette. Has anyone reading this not yet learned the hard way to take care when replying to "All," or when typing addresses (especially if your e-mail host automatically completes an address after you supply the first couple of letters)? We've all had misadventures in the minefield of e-mail: we've been misunderstood when we sent a brief and artless message. We've embarrassed ourselves with typos, crashed our recipients' computers with oversize attachments, and infected friends and loved ones with cyber diseases. That the potential for offense and personal humiliation through the misuse of e-mail is vast and terrifying is well known. But I can suggest some points of e-mail etiquette that will help you avoid misunderstanding, annoyance, and disaster.

First, on forwarding messages: it's not polite to forward a colleague's message without asking, unless your established work arrangement with that person gives you implicit permission. Even then, you must be very careful. I was once dismayed when one of my coworkers forwarded our accumulated correspondence about a production issue to a consultant outside the company, forgetting that at the beginning of the correspondence I had written something graceless and impatient about that person ("Whosit wants such-and-such. What should I tell her?"). Another time, an acquiring editor forwarded my initial evaluation of a manuscript to the author. My notes had been written for an in-house meeting, pointing out the clumsy word processing, the various cleanup chores the manuscript would require, and a list of unresolved issues, without any mention of the project's virtues. It was certainly not how I would have chosen to introduce myself to that author. Another courtesy when forwarding is to make sure first that the recipient hasn't already been copied on the message. One of my superiors regularly forwards mail to me that I've already received, which not only adds clutter to my in-box, but also causes the occasional confusing déjà vu.

Second, it's impolitic to copy an e-mail to people other than the person you're nudging. Only under desperate circumstances should you do this, after you've tried more than once unsuccessfully to get a response from the person herself. It's especially mean to copy in the supervisor of the delinquent before she has a chance to explain what's going on. I can think of several times recently when I've been embarrassed or annoyed by the public airing of my mistakes—fairly or unfairly—in group e-mails.

Even when the issue doesn't involve a problem, the inclusion of my boss in an e-mail to me on an innocuous topic suggests that the sender thinks I require supervision in the matter. One of my authors had a habit of copying the acquiring editor when he replied to my queries, and as a result I was reluctant to e-mail him at all. He didn't realize that I didn't necessarily want anyone else to read the kinds of things I was struggling with in his manuscript. I have a freelancer who always sends his bill to my boss, never mind that she then has to send it on to me. And that I then have to copy and process it and give it back to her. The whole thing is almost funny when you think about it. But it still gets up my nose. Am I overly sensitive? Possibly—but if I am, no doubt others are, too, so take that into account when you go public with what might better remain a private exchange.

Third, on replying: if your settings don't automatically include the sender's original message, make it clear what it is you are replying to. It's anywhere from aggravating to alarming to receive a cryptic message from someone you queried days ago where the subject line is "IMPORTANT!" and the answer is something like "Yes—thanks—critical! Please do immediately."

Finally, on e-mail you initiate: set up your automatic signature to include full contact information. Who uses a phone book these days? I like to click on someone's latest e-mail message and find what I need at the bottom of it. When it's not there, it's not always easy to locate the information elsewhere.

WORKING THROUGH CHANNELS, NOT OVER HEADS

Above, I gave the examples of asking Linda personally whether she could crank out the report on time and asking Mrs. R. for a talk about how to work better together. In both cases, the point was to address the person most responsible, and that person alone. In similar scenarios, however, I've been copied in on e-mails to the entire team to the effect that "FYI, Linda, the Henry project is now in danger of missing the conference date." No reasons are mentioned, but the damage is done—everyone thinks that Linda is responsible. Did the sender know that Linda received the final e-files only yesterday? Checking in personally with Linda before sending the note might have helped the sender phrase the group e-mail more diplomatically.

When copy circulates through an office and people make corrections and sign off on it, there's a special temptation to show up someone who defiles your copy. A magazine editor friend of mine recalls the time she got copy she'd edited back from a superior who had "corrected" Aaron Copland's name, writing, "It's Copeland!!!" in the margin. Incensed, my friend wrote, "It may be pronounced 'Copeland!!!' but it's spelled 'Copland,'" and rerouted it, humiliating the more senior editor. Although I have a feeling my friend still gets some evil pleasure from that memory, the senior editor's arrogance contributed to a long-standing coolness toward her on the part of the copyediting pool.

"Working through channels" sometimes refers generally to playing by the rulebook rather than doing your own loose-cannon thing. But it more particularly can mean solving a problem by starting with the person who's primarily responsible and not going over his head until all else fails.

Recently I received a poorly written index for an important rush book from a relatively new freelancer. Looking at the disaster, mental alarms sounded: (a) Bad indexer! (b) Delay! (c) Cover tail! Given that those thoughts ripped through my brain in seconds, I was out of my chair and halfway out the door on my way to the managing editor before I stopped and rethought. Instead, I took the index to the acquiring editor, who was familiar with the content of the book and could confirm that it wouldn't do. Then I went back to my computer, redlined some of the pages, and e-mailed them to the freelancer, explaining the problem. I asked him to rework the index, and I told him of the urgency. A little while after sending it, I phoned him. The indexer had understood immediately, made some embarrassed apologies, and promised to fix everything as quickly as possible. Within twenty-four hours, he delivered an excellent revision.

In my mind, there were four beneficiaries of this tactic of addressing a problem at its root: I got my index, only one day late. The freelancer furthered his education. The managing editor had one less headache to tend to. And the reader gained an index that was truly useful. As a bonus, because the indexer demonstrated intelligence and cooperation in his quick and expert revision, I will continue to work with him, so the Press didn't lose a freelancer.

One last reminder: working through channels entails e-mail etiquette as well. Giving thought before forwarding messages or copying people in can save your target some embarrassment and prevent trivial problems from escalating into personal vendettas.

EDITORIAL DISAGREEMENTS

At the top of this chapter, I gathered a bouquet of complaints that are surely familiar to anyone who edits as part of a group effort. Negotiating editing issues with colleagues is not really very different from negotiating with authors. The main differences are that (1) you share a style with your colleagues, and (2) you see them every day in the restroom (well, half of them anyway).

Because your style guide is an accepted arbitration tool in your office, that should be your first stop on the way to resolving editorial differences. If you've made a decision to depart from style, you might have to persuade someone of the reasons. One of my colleagues recently did so—the one whose author wanted to uppercase her job title on the book jacket. I lowercased it on the routing copy, and he e-mailed to plead his case. His message was a model of tact and flattery, all the way down to the smiley face at the end:

> Hi, Carol—I noticed that you, correctly, made the job title lowercase on the jacket. The author had requested that we capitalize her title and since it was part of a package of requests and complaints, most of which I wasn't able to accommodate, I figured it wouldn't hurt to let her have her way on this. I know it's wrong and I'm sure I argued with her about

it during the catalog copy stage (and won), but would you mind if we eschewed Chicago style on this? If you do mind—and I respect that—I'll just pretend I didn't notice. Thanks. ☺

This made me wonder just how difficult this guy thinks I am, but he certainly made it easy for me to agree.

In cases of serious disagreement, look again at the strategies listed in chapter 4 for working with a writer: examine your motives for resisting; use tact in stating your case; let it go if it's more a question of preference than correctness; and as a last resort, appeal to a higher authority. And if the disagreement is with that higher authority? Assigning editors or bosses count as people and colleagues, too, only bigger and more powerful ones. Argue as much as the relationship will bear before you give in graciously. If you end up feeling forced to accept something that's flat-out wrong, file away some evidence of your efforts to correct it. And if that file begins to fatten, think about moving on.

TAKING RESPONSIBILITY

In an office atmosphere where your first instinct is to take cover when something goes wrong, you can help foster a more collaborative culture by owning up when you're the one who's responsible. People respond well to this. In their relief to be off the hook, they tend to be generous—they might offer reassurance or even share the blame. When you say "I'm sorry—I should have caught that," the response is likely to be "Well, we all should have caught it."

If you worry that people are blaming you for something that wasn't your fault, little good can come from laying blame elsewhere. If you think it's important to set the record straight, a low-key query to the person whose opinion you value most might be appropriate. ("I'm not sure exactly what happened here, but I'd like to know so it doesn't happen again. Could we figure it out when you have a minute?") Anger and defensiveness might deflect blame in the moment, but they won't enhance your reputation or ease future transactions with your colleagues.

If you have to work closely with someone who regularly causes trouble for you, try to take the high road, if you can, in order to get along. A friend of mine who was responsible for the final proofreading at a suburban Philadelphia newspaper in the 1970s remembers an eccentric composing-room foreman whose solution when copy didn't fit the page was to slice off the extra lines or paragraphs with his X-Acto knife and toss them in the trash. If it happened to be in midsentence, he would stab in a period with a felt pen. My friend spent a lot of time rummaging in the waste bin to find out how the stories ended and then begging the guy to let her edit some sense into his results. True, there are a few reasons why this arrangement wasn't ideal. But she kept her job without costing him his, and the readers got mostly readable stories.[1]

COVERING YOUR TAIL

In spite of all your good-natured, together, supercollegial coping strategies, there may come a time when you're in the hot seat and you are forced to account for yourself. Maybe a big mistake cost major money. Maybe the company suffered a public humiliation. Maybe the photo of a society matron at the spring fund-raiser accidentally ran with the caption meant for the photo of the peacock spreading its plumes: "This old bird crawled out from behind a rock at the zoo to bask for a while in the warm spring sunlight." (A friend swears this happened at a newspaper where she worked.) When signs point to its being your fault, you will be asked to explain.

1. In this book, my advice will be confined to editorial dustups. If a troublemaker at your workplace crosses the line into sexual harassment, bullying, or other inappropriate or dangerous behaviors, you may need a bigger book than this one, as well as help from your supervisor or human resources department.

How aggressively you defend yourself is something you'll have to decide, but in order to have the choice, you have to have the means, and that's where your schedules, logs, lists, and folders come in handy. Somewhere in there is evidence that will allow you to reconstruct the timing and sequence of events, who notified whom, and what the exact instructions were. And because of your habitual organizing of all that information, you'll be able to find everything you need.

But use it wisely. Control your impulse to e-mail the evidence to twenty people or march into the manager's office waving the printouts in triumph. If other people are stomping about demanding explanations, your ability to stay calm and rational may keep things from escalating. "I've looked at what happened, and I don't see how I could have done anything to prevent it. But if it was my fault, I'd like to understand how."

Of course, if your research shows that you screwed up big-time, it's also your decision whether to own up. I'm for it. "I made a big mistake" might not be easy to say, but if you don't have to say it very often, your reputation won't suffer, especially if you can follow up with your plan for making sure it never happens again.

KEEPING TRACK OF SUCCESS

I know I said we're not in it for the glory—but I lied. One of the nicest rewards of the copy editor's life is when a writer is grateful and bothers to say so in a public acknowledgment. You can bet someone in your workplace will hear about it if the author has problems with your editing. That's why, when you get positive feedback about your work, whether in print or in an e-mail, you should save a copy for your "brag file." Our managing editor reminds us regularly to pass along author compliments to her—she keeps a file that comes in handy when she wants to talk with her own boss about budgeting for promotions and raises.

In your own modest style, you can promote yourself. If you are subjected to an annual performance review, you will probably be asked to make an accounting of your successes over the last year. Or perhaps as a freelancer you depend on a résumé when scouting clients. So make a note of your achievements as they happen and add them to the file. If you brought in a difficult project on time, kept your projects within budget, edited an award-winning piece, worked well on a team effort, increased the amount of editing you were able to handle, took work-related classes, attended a conference—all these are worthy of mention at reckoning time.

A / Sometimes that's fine.

A / Sometimes that's fine.

A / Sometimes that's fine.

A / Sometimes that's fine.

A / He's wrong. Good luck.

CHAPTER TEN

The Freelancer's Quandaries

Q / Can you tell how to became an editer?

WORKING FOR YOURSELF—WITH MANY BOSSES

Not all copy editors work in offices; many of you prefer to work on your own from home as independent contractors. Freelancing can be a terrific way of life, once you're up and running with reliable clients and a steady income. Not having to commute or punch a clock gives you the flexibility to be at home with children, travel, write novels, or to do just about anything else that would suffer in the forty-a-week grind. There are obvious drawbacks, of course: no paid vacations or sick leave, no tech support, iffy health insurance. But my topic here is not to debate the pros and cons of freelancing: they're clear enough that in-house editors frequently talk about cutting loose, while freelancers daydream about salaried positions. Needless to say, freelancing is a huge industry that's valued both by editors themselves and by their employers.

Freelancers face most of the same issues that on-staff copy editors do. You have deadlines, overlapping projects, and authors with personalities. You use the same software, fight the same compulsions. You might even have to work with colleagues or employees, if your business has expanded beyond just yourself. But there are also differences, and they aren't trivial.

The most obvious difference is that freelancers are likely to be paid by several clients, each of whom has a different stylebook or set of procedures for preparing manuscripts. For this reason, your record-keeping must be thorough and well organized. Even if some of your employers give you only occasional work, they won't expect to retrain you each time; it's up to you to keep track of the way they want things done—which dictionary they use, which style guide, the exceptions to the guide. Since another major difference of freelancing is that you compete with other freelancers for work, if you're high maintenance, you lose.

QUANDARY 1: WHEN IT RAINS AND POURS— ACCEPTING COMPETING PROJECTS

Freelancers don't usually set schedules and deadlines. An editor will phone or e-mail to ask about your availability, and she'll tell you the deadline and the number of hours of editing that's been estimated for the job. If she's desperate to find someone, and you aren't available or can't work enough hours per week to meet her deadline, she might agree to change her schedule to accommodate yours. But if you need the work, and you don't detect desperation in her query, you might not be willing to risk losing the job by trying to negotiate. So here's your first quandary: you can either be honest and say you aren't free and lose the job, or you can say "Sure—I'd love to do it" and lose sleep trying to deliver.

This is one way that even seasoned freelancers get themselves into trouble. Supervising editors are faced with the result of this all the time: the freelancer phones or e-mails to say that the manuscript will be late. A smart project editor pads her schedule to allow for some lateness, but that isn't always possible—and even when it is, it doesn't mean she won't be annoyed or remember your tardiness the next time she's hiring. It's better to be up front about your availability and productivity. Make yourself aware of the average number of hours per week you devote to editing, and don't be afraid to quote it to an inquiring editor to see if she can rework her schedule around it. If you develop a reputation as slow but reliable, it will still be a good reputation. You won't be given certain rush jobs, but you'll be at the top of an editor's list for work that has a flexible schedule. (If you develop a reputation as someone who's always late, you won't get the rush jobs, anyway.) There's room for a variety of work styles on an editor's freelancer list, but in her mind, reliability and good work will trump speed for any project where speed isn't an issue.

QUANDARY 2: WHO TAKES THE HIT WHEN THE ESTIMATE GOES WRONG?

Experienced copy editors know the second quandary well: you've contracted for a project, and you're working along in it, and at some point that number of estimated hours begins to look w-a-y too low. The possibility of tardiness is looming, and even if you're able to put in some overtime and meet your deadline, there's the question of whether it's wise for you to charge for many more hours than were estimated. You're on the honor system—there's no way your client will know whether you actually worked the number of hours you claim. You're thinking that if you put down the true number of hours you worked, you won't be believed; you'll be perceived as inflating your bill. Your dilemma: either displease the client by charging more than she budgeted for the job, or short yourself, having worked a number of hours you won't get paid for.

I'm guessing that many more freelancers cheat themselves than cheat their employers when they face this choice. (One experienced freelancer tells me that she long ago gave up keeping track of her hours at all—she just bills the amount that was estimated.) But before you short yourself, consider carefully why the project took longer than estimated. Ask yourself the following two questions:

Question 1. Did the project involve a task that you hadn't met before and had to figure out how to do? When you're new at copyediting, there will be a learning period. Although it's not fair to make one employer pay for that, to a small degree it is fair for an employer to tolerate your learning curve as an investment in future collaborations, in the same way they invest in new in-house editors. If the task was a basic, routine chore that you can expect to dispatch quickly in future manuscripts, absorb the greater cost of learning it yourself. If it was a bit tricky and not necessarily something you would expect to find in most manuscripts, split the difference and bill for half the extra time. If the task was something extraordinary that even a veteran editor would have had to puzzle out and that is unlikely to occur in future manuscripts, bill the client for those hours, along with an explanation.

Question 2. Was the overtime really necessary, or was it the result of your slowness or compulsions? If you didn't know how to change all the British punctuation to American with a few keystrokes and decide to change them all one by one instead, it's not fair for someone else to pay for what amounts to your ignorance or poor judgment. You could have asked someone how to automate the task, and you could have checked with the supervising editor to find out whether it needed doing in the first place. Some chores that amount to cleanup can be done by the typesetter, and all you need to do is note them.

QUANDARY 3: WHEN THE PIPER WANTS PAID—
SETTING AND COLLECTING FEES

Perhaps the most vexing issue for freelancers is money. In-house editors take a paycheck for granted. On your own, however, it may seem as though you live with your hand out. What's more, you're constantly wondering whether you've asked for too little or too much. It reminds me of when I was fourteen and learned that all the other babysitters were getting a flat fee of five dollars for New Year's Eve. I knew I was underpaid at fifty cents an hour—that rate hadn't changed since my mother was in high school—and the family I worked for were constantly coming up short when it was time to pay. So when Mrs. Stubee inquired about New Year's Eve, I told her about the special rate. To my amazement, she agreed. But wouldn't you know—they left me with the children at six that evening and didn't come home until five in the morning. Eleven hours, and Mr. Stubee triumphantly paid me five dollars, not a penny more. Obviously, I've never gotten over it, although at least it taught me the concept of a minimum rate.

How much to charge. As a businessperson providing a service, it's your prerogative to set the rate and your client's obligation to inquire what it is. After that, all parties are entitled to negotiate. The trick is to learn what a reasonable wage is for (1) your level of experience, (2) the service you're offering, and (3) the employer you're working for. These are all separate concerns. After all, a beginning editor should not expect the same pay as an experienced one; a proofreader of fiction should not expect to earn as much as a copy editor of a technical manual; and you can't expect the same wage from a children's book publisher as you would get from a publisher of medical textbooks.

Finding your level will require a little homework. Do some research online at websites for freelancers like that of the Editorial Freelancers Association.[1] Ask the members of your listserv to suggest a range of fees for someone with your level of experience. Or, if you're really stuck, you can ask your new employer straight out what she would normally pay someone in your position. You can say (if it's true), "I believe my experience puts me in the middle of your range." Ask for the top rate only if you're sure your résumé supports it and you know you will deliver top-rate services. You might fear that letting someone else suggest a rate is a good way to get lowballed, but think of it merely as a starting point for negotiation. I believe that most supervising editors will be fair—they want to find and keep good freelancers—but if, based on your research (or your needs), the figure seems low, ask, "Could you manage [X dollars more]?" If the answer is no, you get to decide whether to accept the job or not.

One of my colleagues who does freelance developmental editing in addition to copyediting stresses that although some jobs are worth

---

1. Editorial Freelancers Association: http://www.the-efa.org/res/rates.html.

more than others, a client won't necessarily realize that. She told me that she isn't shy about educating employers who don't understand the value of her services. "If it's simply proofreading, then the costs can remain low. If you are saving them from themselves in a public forum that could potentially make or break their reputations, then the price should be higher."

Raking it in. Ideally, once your routines are established, collecting payment will take care of itself. At the start of a job, get something in writing in the form of a purchase order or a contract. If you work for someone who doesn't bother with such formalities and you're comfortable with that, at the very least you must keep a record of the agreement, and it's wise to send an e-mail confirming the terms before you begin, at least until you've established a working relationship with that person or institution. When you're just starting out in editorial freelancing, it's tempting to ask for partial payment up front. If the employer is an individual (as opposed to an institution) whose creditworthiness has yet to be proven, this might be a smart move, but otherwise it isn't customary. More common is the practice of sending a partial invoice when the work is partly finished, although this is usual only for projects that take more than a couple of months. It's fine to ask your employer about this.

When you're finished editing, you can either send an invoice with the completed work or wait for the client to acknowledge receipt of the work and satisfaction with it. But don't wait more than a couple of days. Prompt billing is essential to maintaining a steady income as a freelancer.

Occasionally freelancers ask me whether I will reimburse their printing costs, or if I could print out the editing myself and mail it to the author. These might be standard procedures at some houses, but I expect freelancers to take care of printing and to fold the cost of paper and ink into their hourly rates. On the other hand, I do expect to receive receipts for postage. It's the difference between estimated costs (which you should absorb) and measurable costs (for which you have receipts). Perhaps more important, it's the difference between performing independently (printing and mailing things yourself) and bothering your manager with tasks she thought she had delegated to you. It's good to sort out such matters before you begin, but if you find yourself out a few dollars for postage or printing, I would rather you quietly add a half hour to the bill than bother me with receipts.

Finally, keep a careful log of your income. Once you earn over a set amount, the federal government will want to know about it. Since no one is withholding taxes from paychecks for you, you'll have to estimate your taxes and make quarterly payments toward them.[2]

Dealing with deadbeats. Fortunately, most of the freelancers I know have little trouble with nonpayment. Many have experienced delayed payments, however, so unless you have other ways to pay the mortgage, you'll have to stay on top of your accounts receivable. If thirty days pass with no response to an invoice, it's accepted business behavior to squeak your wheel: send an e-mail with a copy of the invoice and ask nicely whether the check is in the mail. Squeak as needed until you experience relief. In the rare event that all fails, you might have to threaten to take your complaint to a small claims court. That sounds drastic, but it's more polite and more legal than hiring a couple of burly guys.

YOU'RE NOT ALONE

Although as a freelancer you might literally work at home alone, a community of fellow editors is as close as your keyboard or phone. When you have doubts or questions about a manuscript, reach out to the appropriate resource.

If you have an assigning or supervising editor, she is paid to monitor your progress and answer questions about what she wants. It's more helpful if you organize your queries into occasional batches than if you constantly bombard her, but you can be sure she would rather answer an e-mail from you now and then than sort out the mess later

---

2. Learn more at http://www.irs.gov/taxtopics/tc554.html, or, in plainer English, at http://turbotax.intuit.com/tax-tools/the_self_employment_tax/article.

when the manuscript is on her desk. Feedback from supervisors is also an essential part of your education, so make it a habit to ask for it.

If you live in a city, there might be an organization of freelancers who share information and contacts. Getting involved with such a group will give you opportunities to talk shop, do some networking, and draw on the resources of others.

If you're stuck on a question about basic editing, do the homework yourself. If you can't find help in your style guide or dictionary, check online. Use electronic bookmarks to keep online reference works handy. For those times when you have all the information you need but can't seem to make a decision, join a listserv of copy editors who help each other with editing problems. You'll be amazed at the community you find there—in fact, you'll wonder how anyone gets any work done hanging out at the cyber water cooler all the time. And don't forget—you can always shoot a question to Chicago's Q&A.

A / Probably not.

CHAPTER ELEVEN

The Zen of Copyediting

Q / Contracts often employ defined terms in quotes and parentheses, e.g., ABC Corp. (the "Seller") shall sell ten widgets to XYZ Corp. (the "Buyer"). When drafting such a contract, I always put a period after the close parenthesis if it is the end of the sentence, such as in the above example. But it's like listening to nails on a chalkboard to me to have a period essentially (ignoring the parenthetical) follow the period employed in an abbreviation. What do you recommend?

THE X-TREME EDITOR

There's a stereotype of the copy editor: mousy with thick glasses, dateless and shy, obsessively tidy, relentless in our quest for power over our manuscripts. I once told my son John that I didn't think I was cut out for the job because I got too upset when an author disagreed with something I considered nonnegotiable. When I added that I stuck with it because I couldn't think of any other job I was as suited for, he said, "Maybe you could be a terrorist."

Hmm. Copy editor . . . terrorist . . . are we really as twisted as all that? Sometimes I wonder. One freelancer I asked to do light editing returned a manuscript dripping with red, confessing that he "couldn't help it." The next time I hired him, he did it again. Both times, when sending his invoice, he mentioned that he had actually worked quite a few more hours than he was billing me for, and both times I felt that it was obvious why, so I didn't encourage him to bill for the whole amount. Not only was it awkward wondering whether he felt I was taking advantage of him, but I noticed on the second manuscript that while he had been fiddling with all that rewriting, he had actually missed a few typos and misspellings.

Another editor, a colleague, admitted to me recently that before she learned how to change all the underlining in a manuscript to italics, she highlighted each one and changed it by hand. She knew it wasn't necessary—that the typesetter would do it—but she did it anyway.

Of course I've already confessed my own little compulsion, in that endnote numbers scandal. And let's not even talk about my e-mail filing system.

When I use the word "compulsive," I don't mean to suggest that copy editors suffer more than others from obsessive-compulsive disorder, which is an extreme and disabling illness. Rather, I'm talking about our propensity for meticulousness and perfectionism, traits that are important to us, and which in fact draw us to careers in manuscript editing in the first place. The problem is that there's no end to the amount of fussing you can do with a manuscript, whereas there's a limit to the amount of money someone will pay you to do it. At some point it has to be good enough, and you have to stop.

WORKING TO RULE

It's common for an editing project to be assigned an estimated number of hours. At Chicago, we have various formulas for estimating, but we're aware that they're rough guides. It's difficult to guess what kinds of issues might slow the editing until we're well into the manuscript. Regardless, experienced editors know that there are two kinds of projects: (1) the kind that deserves no more than the estimated number of hours, and (2) the kind that takes however long it takes. The problem is, how do you know which kind you're doing, and if it's type 1, how do you "work to rule"?

If you are a freelancer and you're offered a flat fee for a project, you can assume that the estimated number of hours is what you're expected to give it, and not much more. If you're being paid by the hour, it's usually easy enough to get a sense of a project's importance by asking the assigning editor. ("If I find that it's taking longer than estimated, is that okay?") It's not that you'll ever get him to say that a manuscript is low priority and doesn't need to be perfect. Rather, he will stress its importance if it's the kind of project that he's willing to invest more resources in. He will always want to know if you run into difficulties with a project, but in some instances he'll be quicker to advise ignoring a time-consuming problem.

Working to a specified number of hours is a skill that develops with experience. When you start a project, divide the total number of estimated project hours by the number of working days before the deadline. This will tell you how many hours a day you are expected to put in. If you can't manage that many hours per day, perhaps because you are dividing your days among multiple projects, let the assigning editor know right away that the schedule isn't going to work for you. (And if you're a newbie, be conservative in guessing how many hours you'll last before falling face-first into the monitor—it might surprise you that few people can sit and edit eight hours a day.)

Next, figure out how many pages an hour you ought to be editing in order to finish in the specified number of hours. Here's how to do it. Start with the number of estimated hours. If the estimate includes cleanup, subtract about 15 percent to get the number of hours for editing. (Subtracting 15 percent is the same as multiplying by .85, if that's easier.) Next, divide the number of manuscript pages by the number of estimated project hours to see how many pages per hour you should be editing. You can then multiply the number of pages per hour by the number of hours per day to find out how many pages a day you should aim for.[1]

1. For more depth and precision on this, take a look at a chapter of a book written by the folks at the *Editorial Eye*: "Estimating Editorial Tasks: A Five-Step Method," in *Stet Again! More Tricks of the Trade for Publications People; Selections from "The Editorial Eye"* (Alexandria, VA: EEI Press, 1996).

Monitor your progress. After a few days, if you're on or ahead of target, fine. But if you're taking too long, make some adjustments. Figure out what's slowing you down and how you can economize. You might decide to live with a style that isn't perfectly in line with yours, if it's logical and consistent. (This might involve undoing some editing you've already done.) If you've been straying from spell-checking into fact-checking, dial it back. Sometimes checking facts is part of the job, but often we do it merely because we can't resist. Resist. If you've been writing long-winded queries or taking detailed style notes, try to labor less over them. If you've been going online to check the author's citations or find missing information, stop doing her job. Query instead. Read faster. Look again at my chapter 6: are you wasting time on tasks that you could automate, delegate, or reevaluate?

Nonediting tasks can also be big time-suckers. If you're juggling several manuscripts at different stages of production, reexamine your habits and procedures to see where you can trim. I remember a point a few years ago when I decided I would stop checking whether page-proof spreads aligned across the bottoms of the pages. At the time, I was swamped with proofs from more than one book that arrived on my desk all at once (how does that happen, when we turn in the manuscripts weeks apart?), and I realized that I was taking too long with them. So I decided not to check the alignment. After all, the designer would look for that on his pass through the proofs, and its importance to the reader was slight.

You could say I made a conscious decision to lower my standards. I felt a little guilty. As I wrote that last paragraph, I could almost hear your cries of protest. "No! Anything but that! Don't make us lower our standards!" But let's not be silly. Some of our "standards" are just time-consuming habits that don't really make a difference to the reader. Letting go of them gives us time for more important tasks—and if working for our employers means working to a schedule, working for the reader means using the time we have in the best ways possible. So prepare yourself for the second use of extended italics for emphasis in this book: *The manuscript does not have to be perfect.*

So how subversive is that? Not very. The manuscript does not have to be perfect because perfect isn't possible. There's no Platonic ideal for that document, one "correct" way for it to turn out, one perfect version hidden in the block of marble that it's your job to discover by endless chipping away. It simply has to be the best you can make it in the time you're given, free of obvious gaffes, rid of every error you can spot, rendered consistent in every way that the reader needs in order to understand and appreciate, and as close to your chosen style as is practical.[2]

HANDLING STRESS BEFORE IT ESCALATES

If you're freaking out over the amount of work you have or deadlines that are piling up or a temporary inability to concentrate because of distractions in your personal life, identify the problem and do something about it. If it's a persistent problem, examine your habits and resolve to make some changes. If it's something more particular and immediate, you might have to ask for help in managing the work.

The solution might be to put in some extra hours or take work home. Or see a therapist, or get more sleep, or talk to a friend, or watch a funny movie. (My friend Sarah swears by her CD soundtrack of *Chitty Chitty Bang Bang*.) The important thing is to find a way to shine some light on the end of the tunnel.

You might be reluctant to confide in your manager that you need help, and it's not something you'll want to do very often, but in truly desperate times, a reasonable boss won't hold it against you if you end up whining a little or even falling apart. Some bosses are more tuned in to your state of being than others, which is bad if you'd rather not share, but good if you need the support. When I was experiencing

2. One of my colleagues has some advice for the overzealous: when she is worried about mistakes in proofs and realizes that the author has done a slapdash job and not actually proofread, she tells herself, "You can't care more about the book than he does," and stops herself from reading the proofs for him.

a bad patch a few years ago, my boss e-mailed to say that I seemed "subdued" lately, or some such euphemism. I didn't think my work had been suffering, but I apologized in case it had. He wrote back that everything was fine, but urged me to "take some time off if you need it" and reminded me that human resources was there to help. Exactly the appropriate response—supportive but not prying, and keeping professional boundaries intact. It moved me to take action to get myself back on track, although I wished at the time that I'd done it without prompting.

HAVE A LIFE

Put briefly, the way to bring your best to any job is to have a life away from the job. Good copy editors are liberally educated and culturally literate.[3] They know a foreign language or two, are reasonably numerate, and have traveled a bit. If you listen to music, read novels, raise pets or children or vegetables, rehab your house, or attend *Star Trek* conventions, I believe you'll be a better worker for it.

Ultimately, if you bring your best to your work knowing that the manuscript is not your life, you'll understand why one former colleague and mentor was not lowering her standards or abandoning responsibility when she used to counsel us "Remember—it's only a book."

How deliciously subversive.

A / Yoga?

3. When I applied for my first job in academic publishing, at the University of Illinois Press, the test included having to identify a list of famous people. An editor there who was a friend of mine had once told me about taking the test, long before she knew I'd one day apply for that job. She was embarrassed that she hadn't recognized the name of one of the U.S. presidents. I forgot all about it until I was taking the test and came to a name I didn't know—so I wrote that it was a U.S. president. I hope it was. In any case, I got the job and sent flowers to my friend.

You *Still* Want to Be a Copy Editor? Breaking In

It's a truism that to get a job that will give you experience, you need experience, and unfortunately editing jobs are no exception. With copyediting increasingly outsourced to freelancers, large in-house departments are becoming more rare, and the kind of apprenticeships we used to serve at the feet of a watchful veteran may not be as easily available, but it's still common for hiring supervisors to mentor freelance editors with the aim of maintaining a stable of dependable employees.

Here at Chicago we are always looking for good freelancers, but for us to hire you we require that you have experience copyediting scholarly books, and we ask you to take an editing test as well. Newspapers and magazines routinely follow the same drill.

So how do you get started?

One strategy, if you are young enough that your parents won't notice, is to move back home for a while and volunteer at a publishing company as an unpaid intern. When I worked in children's books, we had a series of interns, most of whom went on to find paid positions on the strength of their work for us and the recommendations we gave them. If you can't live at home, you might try to volunteer for a few hours a week, if your other job permits. As an intern, you can do certain chores, like proofreading, evaluating unsolicited manuscripts, or updating e-files of edited manuscripts, which will give you a feel for editing marks and an introduction to proofing. Proofreading can be especially instructive if you are given the edited manuscript to proof against, since it will give you a chance to see and learn from the editor's corrections and queries. If you're smart and learn fast, your supervisor might be willing to recommend you for proofreading jobs elsewhere, which is a big step toward working as a copy editor.

Although many universities offer degrees in journalism, an alternative is a shorter-term course in publishing, like the one at Columbia University in New York City. A less expensive strategy is to take a class in manuscript editing. For instance, the University of Chicago offers a certificate in manuscript editing through its Graham School of Continuing Education. There are also online courses you can take. If you're a good student, the teacher can be a resource for finding job openings and might be willing to give you a recommendation when you finish the class. Since many employers of copy editors require you to take a test, an editing class will also help prepare you for that.

If you can get work proofreading, you might be able to use that as a stepping-stone to work as a copy editor. If you happen to be knowledgeable in a specialized area of math or science or fluent in a foreign language, you'll be a prime candidate for this, so be sure to mention it on your applications. If you get a nibble, the next step will probably be a proofreading test, so prepare yourself for that by learning proofreaders' marks and practicing on your friends' term papers and dissertations. *The Chicago Manual of Style* or another relevant style guide can be bedside reading at this stage. If you're able to say that you're already familiar with a particular style—such as Chicago, or AP, or MLA—you'll look better to a hiring editor. As a proofreader, you might be able to build a relationship with a supervising editor willing to ease you gradually into copyediting.

If you can find even just one job freelance copyediting, and then build on that to accumulate the experience of copyediting several manuscripts for that employer, it probably will not be difficult to parlay that experience into work for other employers. Many publishers require freelancers to pass an editing test before they will hire them, but at a certain point in your development, they may be willing to hire you on the basis of your experience and references. Some experienced freelancers say that word of mouth is their most effective method of finding new clients.[1]

Finally, there are countless print and electronic resources out there for you to explore. The Internet is a mine of information for proofreaders and copy editors, whether you're trying to break in or already have years of experience. There are also books filled with tips and resources. You can search for them online or in library databases or in person at your bookstore or library. I'll list a few below to get you started.

I wish you well.

1. "Experienced Editors' Wisdom," Northwest Independent Editors Guild, http://www.edsguild.org/wisdom.htm (accessed August 25, 2007).

Acknowledgments

Sincere thanks to my many mentors and allies in manuscript editing, quite a few of whom could have written this book, and whose anecdotes and advice are at the heart of it: Barbara Bagge, Alice Bennett, Mary Caraway, Erik Carlson, Leslie Cohen, Erin DeWitt, Jean Eckenfels, Kate Frentzel, Jenni Fry, Mary Gehl, Ruth Goring, Teresa Hagan, Russell David Harper, Sandra Hazel, Leslie Keros, Michael Koplow, Mary Laur, Margaret Mahan, Mara Naselli, Susan Olin, Mark Reschke, the late Claudia Rex, Maia Rigas, Anita Samen, Christine Schwab, Joel Score, Edward Scott, Rhonda Smith, Cheryl Solimini, Rebecca Sullivan, Nancy Watkins, Lila Weinberg, Lys Ann Weiss, Laura Westlund, and Yvonne Zipter.

For professional advice and enthusiasm, I am grateful to Laura Andersen, Marc Aronson, Victoria Baker, Kira Bennett, Susan Bielstein, Nathan Bierma, Dean Blobaum, Michael Brehm, Louise Brueggemann, Rosina Busse, Perry Cartwright, Kit Chaskin, Joe Claude, Joan Davies, Lindsay Dawson, Paula Barker Duffy, Joëlle Dujardin, Nanci Erkert, Ann Esse, Clairan Ferrono, Eric Gamazon, Alister Gibson, Ellen Gibson, Kathleen Hansell, Mark Heineke, Diane Herrmann, Rob Hunt, Jaci Hydock, Penny Kaiserlian, Blair Kamin, Carol Kasper, Deborah Brown Kazazis, Charles Lipson, Robert Lynch, Sylvia Mendoza, Jane Miller, Sarah Oaks, Richard Oesterlin, Judy O'Malley, Joseph Parsons, Randy Petilos, Rodney Powell, Chris Rhodes, Jill Shimabukuro, Linda

Erf Swift, Margie Towery, John Tryneski, Joseph Weintraub, Aiping Zhang, and Sara Zimmerman.

I am indebted to Kathy Dorman, Elizabeth Fama, Tiana Pyer-Pereira, John Saller, Ed Scott, and three anonymous reviewers for the Press, all of whom read versions of the manuscript and offered suggestions for improvement and expansion. I am especially grateful to Marilyn Schwartz, a fourth reader for the Press, for her many wise and inspired suggestions. Erin DeWitt, Mara Naselli, Ed Scott, and Lys Ann Weiss gave me special help with the chapter on freelancing. Russell Harper has a special claim to thanks for taking over the editing of the Q&A in January 2001 and maintaining it with expertise and hilarity for nearly three years.

Heartfelt thanks to my writing group—Elizabeth Fama, Kate Hannigan, Linda Hoffman Kimball, and Amy Timberlake—for their cheerleading and tough love, and to Brad Inwood for decades of unflagging encouragement.

My editor, Paul Schellinger, listened, challenged, and tactfully prodded me into shaping and finishing the book. I am grateful for his initial support and continuing encouragement. I am indebted many times over to my managing editor, Anita Samen, for her patience, her sense of humor, and her feisty and effective management style. Erin DeWitt's expert and generous editing improved the manuscript in countless ways; she has my warmest thanks. Sincere thanks, too, to Isaac Tobin and Sylvia Mendoza, who respectively designed and produced these elegant pages.

To my sons, John and Ben, I dedicate this book with love and gratitude.

Further Reading

Allen, David. *Getting Things Done: The Art of Stress-Free Productivity.*
New York: Viking, 2001.

ALWD Citation Manual: A Professional System of Citation. 3rd ed. Edited
by the Association of Legal Writing Directors and Darby Dicker-
son. New York: Aspen, 2006.

The American Copy Editors Society ("A professional organization
working toward the advancement of copy editors in newspapers,
magazines, Web sites and other journalistic endeavors"). At http://
www.copydesk.org/.

The Associated Press Stylebook and Briefing on Media Law. New York: Basic
Books, 2004. Available at http://www.apstylebook.com/.

The Bluebook: A Uniform System of Citation. 18th ed. Cambridge, MA:
Harvard Law Review Association, 2005.

Canadian Guide to Uniform Legal Citation. 5th ed. Toronto, ON: Carswell/
McGill Law Journal, 2002.

*The Chicago Manual of Style: The Essential Guide for Writers, Editors, and
Publishers.* 15th ed. Chicago: University of Chicago Press, 2003.

The Chicago Manual of Style Online. "New Questions and Answers." http://www.chicagomanualofstyle.org.

Copperud, Roy H. *American Usage and Style: The Consensus.* New York: Van Nostrand Reinhold, 1980.

Copyediting: Because Language Matters. Bimonthly newsletter published by McMurry, Inc. Also available at http://wwwcopyediting.com.

Copyediting-L: Stalking Danglers around the World. (A list maintained by Indiana University "for copy editors and other defenders of the English language who want to discuss anything related to editing"). http://www.copyediting-l.info/.

The Editorial Eye. Monthly newsletter published by EEI Communications. Online-only edition at http://www.theeditorialeye.com/.

Editorial Freelancers Association ("The professional resource for editorial specialists and those who hire them"). At http://www.the-efa.org/.

Editorium. http://www.editorium.com/.

Editorium Update. Newsletter ("Provides tips about editing, writing, and typesetting in Microsoft Word") http://www.editorium.com/newsletr.htm.

Editors' Association of Canada/Association Canadienne des Réviseurs ("Promotes professional editing as key in producing effective communication"). At http://www.editors.ca/about_EAC/index.html.

EEI Communications Staff. "Estimating Editorial Tasks: A Five-Step Method." In *Stet Again! More Tricks of the Trade for Publications People; Selections from "The Editorial Eye,"* 279–81. Alexandria, VA: EEI Press, 1996.

Einsohn, Amy. *The Copyeditor's Handbook: A Guide for Book Publishing and Corporate Communications.* 2nd ed. Berkeley: University of California Press, 2005.

E-What? A Guide to the Quirks of New Media Style and Usage: How to Handle Inconsistencies in Punctuation, Capitalization, Internet Addresses, and More. Alexandria, VA: EEI Press, 2000.

"Experienced Editors' Wisdom." Northwest Independent Editors Guild. http://www.edsguild.org/wisdom.htm.

Fowler, H. W. *A Dictionary of Modern English Usage.* 2nd ed. Revised and edited by Sir Ernest Gowers. Oxford: Oxford University Press, 1965.

Gordon, Karen Elizabeth. *The New Well-Tempered Sentence: A Punctuation Handbook for the Innocent, the Eager, and the Doomed.* New York: Ticknor and Fields, 1993.

Gross, Gerald, ed. *Editors on Editing: What Writers Need to Know about What Editors Do.* 3rd ed. New York: Grove, 1993.

Harnack, Andrew, and Eugene Kleppinger. *Online! A Reference Guide to Using Internet Sources.* Boston: Bedford/St. Martin's, 2001.

Hart, Geoff. *Effective On-Screen Editing.* N.p.: Diaskeuasis Publishing, 2007. Available at http://www.geoff-hart.com.

Heslop, Brent, David Angell, and Peter Kent. *Word 2003 Bible.* Indianapolis: Wiley, 2003. (Includes a searchable CD-ROM.)

Judd, Karen. *Copyediting: A Practical Guide.* 3rd ed. Menlo Park, CA: Crisp Learning, 2001.

MLA Style Manual and Guide to Scholarly Publishing. 2nd ed. Edited by Joseph Gibaldi. New York: Modern Language Association of America, 1998.

The New Fowler's Modern English Usage. Rev. 3rd ed. Edited by R. W. Burchfield. New York: Oxford University Press, 2000.

New York Times Manual of Style and Usage. Rev. ed. Edited by Allan M. Siegal and William G. Connolly. New York: Times Books, 1999.

Plotnik, Arthur. *The Elements of Editing: A Modern Guide for Editors and Journalists.* New York: Collier/Macmillan, 1982.

Powers, Hilary. *Making Word Work for You: An Editor's Intro to a Tool of the Trade*. New York: Editorial Freelancers Association, 2007.

Publication Manual of the American Psychological Association. 5th ed. Washington, DC: American Psychological Association, 2001.

Rabiner, Susan, and Alfred Fortunato. *Thinking Like Your Editor: How to Write Great Serious Nonfiction—and Get It Published*. New York: Norton, 2002.

"Resources for Freelance Editors." Northwest Independent Editors Guild. http://www.edsguild.org/resources.htm.

Schwartz, Marilyn. *Guidelines for Bias-Free Writing*. Bloomington: Indiana University Press, 1995.

Scientific Style and Format: The CBE Manual for Authors, Editors, and Publishers. 7th ed. Compiled by the Style Manual Committee of the Council of Science Editors. Reston, VA: Council of Science Editors in cooperation with the Rockefeller University Press, 2006.

Sharpe, Leslie T., and Irene Gunther. *Editing Fact and Fiction: A Concise Guide to Book Editing*. Cambridge: Cambridge University Press, 1994.

The Slot ("A spot for copy editors since 1995"). By Bill Walsh. http://www.theslot.com.

Stainton, Elsie Myers. *The Fine Art of Copyediting*. 2nd ed. New York: Columbia University Press, 2002.

Strunk, William, Jr., and E. B. White. *The Elements of Style*. 4th ed. Boston: Allyn and Bacon, 2000.

Turabian, Kate L. *A Manual for Writers of Research Papers, Theses, and Dissertations: Chicago Style for Students and Researchers*. Edited by Wayne C. Booth, Gregory G. Colomb, Joseph M. Williams, and University of Chicago Press editorial staff. 7th ed. Chicago: University of Chicago Press, 2007.

Tyson, Herb. *Microsoft Word 2007 Bible*. Indianapolis: Wiley, 2007.

The University of Chicago Manual of Legal Citation. 2nd ed. Edited by the staff of the *University of Chicago Law Review* and of the *University of Chicago Legal Forum*. Chicago: University of Chicago, 2000.

The Word MVP Site. http://word.mvps.org/. (Tips and tutorials on using MS Word for PC and Mac. Includes a troubleshooting section.)

Words into Type. 3rd ed. Based on studies by Marjorie E. Skillin, Robert M. Gay, and other authorities. Englewood Cliffs, NJ: Prentice Hall, 1974.

Wyatt, Allen. *Allen Wyatt's Word Tips*. http://WordTips.VitalNews.com. (Well organized to help you find quickly what you need to know.)

Index